The Part That Can't Be Sold

A Father and Son's Memoir of

By
Talbot Harlin
and
Clay Harlin

Written by:
Talbot Harlin
with Clay Harlin

Manuscript edited by:
Anna Floit, The Peacock Quill

Photographs:
Harlin family collection
© Robin Hood

Copyright © 2024 by Clay and Talbot Harlin
All rights reserved. This book, or parts thereof, may not be reproduced in any form without permission.

Published By:
Noble Friend, Franklin, TN
September 01, 2024

This story could not have been possible
without the notable contributions of:

Dan Ford

Johnny Haffner

Jim Hayes

Nor would it be complete without the
days we were privileged to spend with:

Rocky Jones

For more of the story, please visit:

HarlinsdaleFarm.com

Table of Contents

Prologue	7
A June Morning, 1995	15
A June Morning, 1964	23
Bloodlines	29
Down to the Upper Barn	45
Country Horsemanship	51
That Yella Mare with the Red Tag	57
Syrup Lips, alias Dynamic Dan	73
Tougher 'n Tarzan	77
Old Blue and the Boys	85
Automatic Post Hole Digger	103
Harpeth River Submarine	109
It Ain't About Muscle	117
$196	127
The Veteran	131
Heir Apparent	139
Tyrannus Equus Rex	155
The Dance	165
Can't Get Right	181
Clay's Gonna Be Alright	193
The Show	199
The Sale	219
For Such a Time as This	233
Elegy	247

"Make it your ambition to lead a quiet life: You should mind your own business and work with your hands, just as we told you, so that your daily life may win the respect of outsiders and so that you will not be dependent on anybody."

1 Thessalonians 4:11-12

Prologue

This is the story of a place and time that, it seems now, might have only been a dream. It's the story of some men who were in ways fortunate to pass over while the dream was still alive, and the rest of us still living who had to learn to know life without it. It's a story that reaches back a hundred years or more and continues on through my children. They will be shaped by my dream the way I was shaped by my father's, who was shaped by his father and his grandfather.

We will do our best to tell these stories as we remember, as we lived them, and as they have been told to us. Some of it will be smoothed and polished with time and perspective. Some of it will be slightly embellished and devoid of the less palatable details. Some of it is probably not completely true, but none of it is made up. We tell this story for each other, because we can't let it all fade away, losing its sharp edges in our memory as the years go by.

Harlinsdale is gone, the way we knew it anyway, when it had life and motion and purpose. Like the light in the eyes of a loved one who has passed away, the body is still there but its soul is gone and we can never really bring it back. In another way, perhaps a better way, we found that by telling the story to each other, the parts of the farm that were truly valuable are still alive. It turns out that it wasn't the land, or the horses, or the barns. It was the hard work it demanded, the people who worked it, and the lessons it taught us.

I think we have all been longing for a way to immortalize it, to clearly define and preserve what the farm meant to us. When I was growing up, Harlinsdale was still ascendant and full of hope. In the summer of '95 we had every stall on the south side of the Show Barn filled with a champion stallion. We were running close to a hundred yearlings through our auction in Shelbyville every August, where our bloodlines could easily fetch $30,000 or more. Our stud fees were upward of $2,500 for a live foal, and via artificial insemination we could breed thirty or forty a day among all our stallions.

We had a team of a dozen or more of my cousins and friends to work the farm, so all the minutiae that made the place beautiful was attended to. The fences were painted bright white, the grass around the barns was mowed and trimmed, the old barns were shorn up, and new barns were built. The iconic Harlinsdale Farm sign with the profile of Midnight Sun was repainted and hung on new posts.

Little did I know back then that Harlinsdale had fewer than ten years to live. By 2004 all the grandchildren had grown up and gone off to live life, and the walking horse industry imploded for a number of reasons. Dad was actually ostracized for a period of time for saying publicly what we all knew to be true—things about the unsound and cruel training practices being used on the "Big Lick" performance walking horses. Trainers and owners pulled their stallions from our barn, clients decided not to bring their mares back to breed that year, and judges at horse shows suddenly saw flaws in our bloodlines[1].

Boycotted is the word, I guess. I was always proud that Dad spoke the truth; I never really cared about any of the Big Lick performance horses, never really understood them. The contest was all too subjective for me. Dad's honesty to a reporter from the Tennessean was less an indictment of the industry than a warning that if they didn't change, they would destroy themselves and our livelihood as a result. In both cases he was right. But the truth is, that's not what killed the farm. It was just time I guess, wear and tear and the world moving on around it. The maintenance of the place alone had become an albatross around our neck.

Almost nothing about Franklin is the same as it was in that summer of '95. There's a Starbucks on the corner of Five Points now. The old Gray Drug Co. storefront is a live music and restaurant venue. Most of the old family farms are now neighborhoods like all the other old farms I knew growing up. The old, cast iron stove factory across from Harlinsdale is now a thriving concert and events venue filled with restaurants and local vendors selling homespun goods.

But to be honest, as much as I lament the change, the city has done a great job of preservation. Where historic sites were butted up against commercial buildings, the city spent tax dollars to reclaim the spaces. Despite the cultural outcry against civil war monuments, Old Chip still stands atop his pedestal on the town square, flanked by four brass "six-pounder" field guns. As I write this, he is still keeping watch over the dead, staring southeast toward the Carter House where John Hood finally wrecked the army of Tennessee.

---

1 The line of champion horses whose characteristics were bred into generations of our yearlings; or the line of ancestors whose characteristics can be found in generations of their offspring.

Harlinsdale itself is probably the most shining example of Franklin's determination to preserve its soul.

Seeing the mounting pressure on the family to keep up the property, combined with the temptation to follow the crowd and sell out to a land developer, the city of Franklin approached my grandfather and his brother Tom with a proposal in 2004. In exchange for selling the property to the taxpayers for a reduced price, they would preserve the farm in perpetuity. The iconic barns would stand, the fences would be painted and maintained, the equine history of the place would be preserved.

In its current form, Harlinsdale is a two-hundred-acre park with rolling hills of green grass, walking trails, riding trails, river access for kayakers, an arena for horse shows, and an amphitheater-style concert venue that has hosted the Pilgrimage Music Festival since 2015. That same big hill where I would run our herd of brood mares back toward the breeding barn now echoes with the sounds of Chris Stapleton, Justin Timberlake, and The Foo Fighters every September.

For me it was never really about Tennessee walking horses; that is to say my love of horses and of our farm had nothing to do with what people traditionally trained Tennessee walkers to do. My great-grandfather was there in the Lewisburg courthouse with his sons in 1935 when the breed was formally registered. In 1944 he and his brother Alex bought a colt no one wanted and turned him into the legendary Midnight Sun, who sired every champion Tennessee walking horse since 1949, save only four. I knew my family was important in that world, but I guess I took it for granted.

At horse shows or around the barn I was introduced as "Clay's boy" and that seemed to mean something to people I had never met. But enough has been written about the history of the Tennessee walking horse breed and the role my family played in it, and I have no desire to recreate it in detail here. Most of what I know of the Tennessee walking horse history and my family's part in it has only taken solid shape in my mind while writing these stories.

When I was younger, I would ride out to Shelbyville with my mom and sisters to see my dad for the last day at "The Sale," our annual yearling auction. This to me was the Big Show. A few dozen spectators, the auctioneer chattering away, my grandfather providing color commentary on each colt or filly. My dad and the other farmhands would be covered in sweat as they took turns running beside a wild-eyed yearling through the auction barn in the August heat.

Later that night we'd go to the other big show, the Celebration championship show. We'd have a box or two for the Harlin family down the show rail, eat cotton candy and fried doughnuts, and watch the classes leading up to the finals. I can still feel the wind sweep past, trailing the smell of horse sweat and leather when the show horses came stepping by, Larry Bright hitting a lick of the Flat Walk Boogie on the organ. The last show always took way too long for a young boy to wait for, long into a night I knew was only going to get longer with an hour ride back to Franklin. Going to the Celebration was part of our family tradition, marking time on the calendar as prominently as any other holiday.

I showed yearlings at horse shows in those summers too, some small shows like Belfast or Spring Hill. I even showed one of our big fall colts at the Celebration one year. My older sister, Anna (or Anna Beth, as we called her), rode some flat-shod walking horses in the pleasure riding classes, and Dad, I'm sure, showed in the saddle a few times for fun. I would see some of our champion studs being exercised around the barn, hitting a few strides of the classic running walk, but our riding horses at the barn were always flat shod or barefoot and I've never actually ridden a Tennessee Walker doing what people now call the Big Lick.

I don't say as of some way to absolve myself from being a part of that unfortunate history, but honestly, I always thought the Big Lick performance horses were strange. It seemed like such an unnatural thing to make a horse do, and for no apparent purpose. It was impressive and looked powerful; I guess I could see that. But I just couldn't imagine a scenario in which I would want to ride around in a tuxedo and tails on a big horse with ribbons in its hair and wearing four-inch lifted shoes.

The fact that the good ole boys' club wanted to go to war with the regulators to preserve this part of the industry is equally baffling to me. It wasn't until I left my bubble in Franklin and moved around quite a bit that I found out how ridiculous it sounded to try and explain to someone why you would make a horse do that. I never really thought much about it in those summers though; it was all part of normal life, and my family's place in the history of the Tennessee walking horse breed is still a source of pride to me now as much as it was then.

But that's still not what Harlinsdale was.

What it was for me may not be what it was for my granddaddy or his dad, or even my sisters or cousins. I think it's something that is personal to us all and it may take more time before some of us can look back on what it was without feeling the pain of losing it.

For me it was a thing far removed from show arenas and bright lights and polished leather tack. It was the smell of the hay loft upstairs in the Show Barn and knowing that my great-grandfather knew that smell too. It was the crunch of the gravel under my boots as I walked the lane with a yearling colt, shoulder pressed against shoulder and soaked with each other's sweat.

It was the subtle quickening of step from one of my buddies or cousins to be first to the tractor to drive to the next barn. It was the sting on my forearms of a hundred tiny cuts from stacking thousands of hay bales. It was the camaraderie of hard work, of being able to say you were there when someone spoke of a hard day. It was the pride of being chosen to do the hard things and finding out you could hack it. It was the quiet moment early in a work day, taking the time to gently approach a foal tucked away behind its momma, and gain its trust just long enough for a chin scratch.

It was knowing you came from something and belonged to it. Not just a story you can tell, or a dream to remember, but something that is ongoing and is still being told.

My memory blends together the things I saw with my own eyes as easily as the stories of people I never met; was never alive to meet. Mr. Hayes passed away a year before I was born, but I knew him. He was there, at the farm. He was there in my dad and Rocky Jones and Dan Ford, and in all the men who told his stories. There was always a direct link between present and past and at fourteen years old it never occurred to me that there may not be a future.

Perhaps, however, this doesn't have to be. We humbly endeavor to see if we can make you feel what it was. To make it live again as you feel the rope burn in your hands, your back ache, and the sweat sting your eyes. To smell the sweet smell of fresh-cut hay in the barn, and feel the dew on the grass of a cool June morning in a Tennessee horse pasture.

We hope those who have gone before us would have been proud of the story we tell, even if they might have remembered it a little differently. We hope that family and friends with their own stories to tell will feel we have done it justice, but such is the risk we take. We hope only to share with you the love of a place that made us who we are, and still has much to give.

-Talbot Harlin

A June Morning, 1995

It was early. Not that early, but too early to be getting up on the first day of summer break. There wouldn't be any Nintendo or MTV for me—there would actually never be a Nintendo in our house and we didn't subscribe to cable TV—but in any case, my summer break was taking a more consequential turn. This was the summer of my fourteenth year, the summer I had been told I could work on the farm. Not just for a few hours on the half day my dad and the guys worked on Saturdays. Not just to spend a Sunday afternoon riding horses or shooting at squirrels up on the Bluff. No sir, that was a young boy's life of leisure and that life was over. I was going to take my place in one of those rickety chairs that lined the entrance to the Show Barn. I was going to be there covered in sweat, lunge line[1] in hand, holding on to an excitable yearling colt barely under control, shoulders slouched under the weight of a long, hard day. I was going to be one of the men like my dad who I had seen all of my life when I came down to the Barn to play.

I was out of bed and dressed by 6:15 a.m., downstairs for breakfast by 6:30. To this day I can't believe the amount

---
[1] A long rope used to do ground work with unbroken horses. A detailed explanation can be found in the story titled, *The Dance*.

of energy I could squeeze out of some cereal or a pop tart or what little water we used to drink during the day. These days I can't make it through an entire morning without a protein bar or some other snack between breakfast and lunch. Years later (come to think of it, not that many years later) I would join the Marines, where we would drain our one-quart canteens every hour in an effort to stave off dehydration. At Harlinsdale we somehow survived on twelve-ounce Mountain Dews from the "cold drink" machine, and my meager breakfast would tide me over until noon.

Dad and I were out the door by 6:50 for the five-minute drive down to the Barn. That's what we always called it when I was a kid. "Can we go down to the Barn after church?" "When's Daddy coming home from the Barn?" *The Barn* was really a two-hundred-acre farm composed of no less than seven barns, ten pastures, half a dozen tractors (not all of which functioned but made for some great pretend B-17 cockpits), and on any given day, over two hundred Tennessee walking horses.

On this day, with our entire stock of last year's foals—yearlings now—plus the spring foaling season underway and all our brood mares toting around a new colt or filly of their own, plus all the boarders on the property for breeding, that number very well could have been beyond three hundred. A quick shortcut down Eddy Lane and Liberty Pike, under the old railroad bridge, right onto Franklin Road, and there it came into sight. Miles of white, wooden fences lining the road and acres of wide-open pasture with lush, green grass. A left turn down the Lane and there it was: the iconic white and green Show Barn of Harlinsdale Farm. The Lane was paved, technically, although it required a fair bit of bobbing and weaving to avoid all the potholes and lumps of asphalt that never got tamped down properly. I'm pretty sure my grandfather, as frugal as he could be, preferred the potholes as effective speed bumps.

There were two paved parking spots in front of the Show Barn, but no one parked there unless you were W. W. "Bill" Harlin, Jr.[2] himself or some uninitiated visitor. To the right of the Lane as you approached the roundabout was Midnight Sun's grave, complete with marble headstone and epitaph, "The Horse of the Century." Everyone parked in the grass under the trees to the left of the lane. There was some sort of system to it that I don't think was ever discussed, but everyone had a specific spot. Everyone left their keys in the ignition, even visitors, just in case trucks and cars had to be moved for some reason like a bush hog in action, or some thirsty fellow slipped you a few bucks and said, "Take my truck up to the store and get us a Gatorade."

Rocky always had an F150 of some vintage, Dad had a Dodge Dakota, and W. L. and Michael had short-bed trucks that I can picture but can't quite make out the brand. Alfred had some sort of Pontiac sedan that he would wedge himself into and Oscar had some old, black Buick-looking thing like a G man from the sixties—but of course Oscar always walked in to work. Granddaddy had a white Ford Bronco just like O. J., except he wouldn't come down to the Barn until later in the morning, as was his prerogative.

In the busy summers the work force would swell to twice its off-season size. In the next summer or two my buddies would join the crew, and my obnoxiously lifted Jeep Wrangler, Martin's Chevy Blazer (until he rolled it fishtailing on an old gravel

---

2 William Wirt Harlin, Jr., my grandfather. Some people were allowed to call him 'Bill' but more formally I heard him referred to as "W. W. Harlin Jr." or simply "Mr. Harlin." William Wirt Harlin, Sr. was my great-grandfather who went by his middle name, Wirt. William "Wirt" Harlin III, was my dad's older brother who sadly passed away in 2012. His son William Wirt Harlin IV is my cousin, referred to simply as "Bill" and worked alongside me at Harlinsdale.

road), and Heath's old diesel F250 would join the menagerie of vehicles parked in the shade in front of that beautiful barn.

In the days before this day there were other characters as well: Homer Ford, his son Clark and his grandsons Dan and Pat, Ben Bowman, Dave Parrish, Al Irwin, Herman MacArthur, Red Laws, Charlie Haffner, Tom Edwards, Chris Ezell, George Massy, Jim Singleton, and Bubba Hay. Then then there was Rocky's brother Bob, Dave Davis, Randy Baker, Dee Hall, Robert Aiken, Leeroy Walker, and Bunny Rabbit. Before Dr. Monty McInturff there was Dr. Johnny Haffner, and Dr. DeWitt Owen before him. Before there was Rocky Jones there was Mr. Hayes—Harlin Hayes, my great-grandfather's nephew—the legendary horseman and original head big man in charge of Harlinsdale. Then of course there was Mr. Hayes' son Jim, my cousins Bill and Tom, Harlin and Mimi, my good friend Aaron Stokes, and Rocky's son Justin.

I'm sure it must have happened once or twice, but for the life of me I can't remember ever beating Rocky to the Barn. In my mind, every time Dad and I turned off the Lane into the grass, Rocky's F150 was already there and he was already in his chair on the marble entryway to the Show Barn.

Finished in 1941[3], this beautiful, eighteen-stall barn was complete with lacquered wood-paneled walls, a massive hay loft that ran the entirety of the second level, and beautiful arched walking bridges to cross over the center aisle between sides of the loft. Flanking the entrance on either side of a ten-by-twenty foot marble walkway were two wood-paneled offices adorned with memorabilia, trophies, and blue ribbons galore. Portraits on the walls of these offices told the story of champion bloodlines dating back to the foundation of the Tennessee walking horse as a breed.

---

3 Completed on December 6, 1941, one day before the Japanese attack on Pearl Harbor.

A June Morning, 1995

The first thing a visitor would see, however, as they cleared the entrance to the Show Barn and stood on that marble slab letting their eyes adjust to the dim light, was the most ridiculous collection of chairs lined up against the opposing walls. Some were old, metal folding chairs replete with rust spots; some were reclaimed outdoor furniture from someone's patio. For a while there was something that resembled an old church pew. None of that seemed remarkable to me at the time, however. All that mattered on that day is that these were the chairs where the men of Harlinsdale sat, and I was going to take my place.

One by one everyone trickled in. To be honest, there was no real objective measure of time at Harlinsdale. You told the time by what you were doing, or what needed to be done, or about what time something usually happened. You didn't start or stop doing something at a specific time, it was just done when it was supposed to be done and it took as long as it took. What time is it? Well, we haven't finished throwing out the Long Barn yet and I haven't seen Monty pull up. Dad and Rocky are still throwing out stalls with us so it must still be pretty early. What time is it? Well, we definitely ate lunch a while ago, and since then I've worked three more colts, so it must be about time to do one more yearling or maybe I'll get told to start feeding.

One day—not this day—I would know I'd proven myself as a horseman when Rocky would correct someone grabbing one of the last colts, "Naw, let Talbot have that one; you go on and start feeding."

The banter across the marble hallway was usually disjointed and halting:

"Y'all see that thing on TV last night?"

"Yeah I saw it."

"Good, huh?"

"Yep."

"You seen that *Braveheart*?"
"Nah 've you?"
"Yeah saw it on Saturdee."
"Reckon Marty'll pick up that mare this mornin'?"
"Nah, he's got one to bring down on Wensdee."
"What'd you think about that back-field?"
"Too wet still."
"Yeah, Tuesdee?"
"Sounds about right."

A lot of what was said sounded like a foreign tongue to an outsider, and if Alfred bothered to speak it would have been in a language all to his own that I did not yet comprehend.

On this day, however, there was something altogether new to talk about. Mr. Harlin's grandson, Clay's boy, was here to be initiated. Thirty years earlier, standing in my footprints would've been Dan Ford or Rocky Jones, Johnny Haffner or my own father, and in those chairs would've sat Mr. Hayes and Homer Ford, Mr. Irwin, Mr. MacArthur, and Dave Parrish. A few years later I would sit on those chairs and watch my younger cousin Harlin and Rocky's son Justin stand in those footprints wearing that same anxious smile. With the same excitement and trepidation felt by those who had gone before us, we all took our seat.

Before I knew anything about being a horseman, I figured a good place to start was a pair of cowboy boots. I didn't know much about being a cowboy and even less about being a horseman, but I did soon learn that the latter profession involved spending a painful amount of time on your feet and not in the saddle. Wearing cowboy boots to a working horse farm was a good way to ruin your boots and your feet. This, of course, was the subject of much cryptic joking that morning that I didn't yet pick up on, along with predictions that the pair of prep-school jeans I had chosen that day would soon be ruined for anything other than having horse manure splattered on them.

Sometime during this banter, if one were to look up the Lane toward Franklin Road you'd see an old man with a broken, bent over gait walking toward the Barn. Shuffle, or maybe hobble, would be a better description of his locomotion.

Oscar lived in one of the old workman's homes on the property, the front door of which couldn't have been more than a hundred yards from the barn. Oscar would take every bit of fifteen minutes to cover that ground. By that I mean the time it took someone to tell a story about something that happened on WWF the night before, a longer discussion about the proper time to rake a hayfield later that week, and a gentlemanly argument about whether or not we should just jump off the old, International tractor with the truck first thing that morning and just leave it running all day, because it's starter was broken (had always been broken as long as I could remember).

Oscar must have been eighty. Some probably untrue—but I'm sticking with it—stories about Oscar involved him getting hit by two separate cars in one night and ending up with two artificial knees. He used to say it was "Mr. Arthur, Arthur Ritus" who hobbled him. One time when pressed if he was "in the war," he told us boys that he drove a bulldozer[4]. I wish to this day I had asked him what he meant by that, but I'm not sure I would have gotten much more out of him. Long before my time, Oscar supposedly bush-hogged Mrs. Hayes' vegetable garden and was summarily fired on the spot. The next day he showed up for work anyway, and the next day and the next.

Here he was again.

---

4 Oscar Pruitt served in the U.S. Army Corps of Engineers.

Oscar's arrival wasn't remarkable except that it seemed to mark some passage of time that was deemed to be adequate. At that moment the banter grew stale, drifted off, and everyone grew quiet and pensive. After a strangely comfortable and appropriate silence, and without any signal that I could ever see, everyone stood up and Rocky said, "Well?" and Dad replied "Yep." And we went to work.

Not that it really mattered, but it was 7:30.

A June Morning, 1964

One early summer day in 1964, an eleven-year-old Clay Harlin, my father, boarded the interurban bus that connected the upscale residential area of south Nashville to the small town of Franklin, about fifteen miles away. His destination was Harlinsdale Farm: two hundred acres of heaven nestled in a bend of the Harpeth River as it flowed west along the outskirts of downtown Franklin, and then turned north until it abutted a formidable limestone rock formation commonly referred to as the Bluff. Its eastern boundary was marked by Franklin Road, or Nashville Pike, depending on your perspective. The northern boundary fluctuated over time but could generally be considered the Spencer Creek waterway.

His grandfather Wirt and his grandmother Luella lived in the antebellum home known as Myles Manor[1] at the southeastern edge of the farm. Dad had been over every inch of that farm as a boy, riding ponies with his cousins, having lunch and lemonade with his grandmother on the porch. He used to strategically position himself by the front door on Saturdays so as not to be left behind when his father would make the trip to

---

[1] This house is referred to as Jasmine Grove in the historic registry, but we always called it Myles Manor. Built in 1836, it served as a U.S. Army hospital after the Battle of Franklin.

Franklin. Today was not about lemonade and ponies, however. Today he was going to work. Or whatever an eleven-year-old boy must have imagined working on a horse farm might look like.

He could not have possibly imagined the consequences of this decision, the life he was about to choose. He could not have imagined the thousands of hay bales he would eventually throw, the literal tons of horse manure he would shovel, and the hundreds of young horses that would try to slam him into barn walls and fence posts, and the ropes they would try to tear from his hands. He definitely had no idea what his innocent eyes would be exposed to on a horse-breeding farm. His father had tried to warn him, something maybe about the birds and the bees, but there really is no way to prepare anyone for that. First things first, he had to get on the bus.

When the driver of the bus spotted him standing alone on Franklin Road, he eased to a stop to let him aboard. Dad's heart thumped in his chest as he looked down the rows of seats to find a spot. There were many adults headed to Franklin for work, but he was the sole eleven-year-old. He chose a seat next to a man who looked pleasant enough, but on closer inspection appeared to have been badly disfigured. His face bore horrible scars that were hard for a young boy to politely ignore. The man noticed Dad's stare and said loudly,

"Boy, what are you looking at?"

This was off to a bad start. My dad wanted to crawl under his seat, but instead he abruptly fixed his gaze straight ahead, never looking at the man again. He made a mental note to look for a kind-faced older lady to sit beside on subsequent trips.

I cannot overstate the determination it must have required for my dad to take this journey. He did not have to work; his family was not in need of any extra income. He had what most people would consider a life of luxury at his home in Nashville. His grandmother would have been content to just have him come and visit for the day; she'd sit on the porch and watch him march off with his .22 into the tree line down by the river and have lunch waiting for him when he returned from his adventure. His grandfather would have indulged any desire he had to come down to the Barn and ride one of his prized Tennessee walking horses, even have one of the farmhands groom and saddle one up for him.

Something else had infected him, though. Something about seeing those men work the farm, the sweat and the satisfaction they wore on their face with honor. The humor and alacrity with which they approached tasks that required them to ignore physical pain and danger. The idea of being handed a saddled-up horse from a real horseman and hearing those words, "Here you go, boy," was something he could no longer abide. If he was going to belong at Harlinsdale Farm, he had to be one of them.

Dad grew up in what he remembers as an iconic snapshot of 1950s America, something out of *Leave it to Beaver* or *Father Knows Best*. By 1964 his father Bill—my grandfather—had established himself in the business world working for his uncle Alex at a garment manufacturing company owned by the two Harlin brothers in Nashville called Red Kap. When Dad was about four years old, his family moved into what he remembers as his childhood home on Robertson Academy Road in Nashville, but he was born at Harlinsdale. For his first three years of life he lived in a house on the edge of the farm just off Franklin Road, next to a stone-walled drive marking the original 1935 entryway that led down to the Hayes' house.

Life in suburban Nashville for my dad was idyllic. It was common to see someone on a horse or a pony, and there were still a few farms around Nashville where his parents could pay a small boarding fee to keep a few of their own horses nearby. There was a lot of love, no fears, plenty of neighborhood to roam in, and a ton of kids to be friends with. Life was just good; good parents, siblings, neighbors, and of course, pets. The kids would walk to school flanked by a frolicking pack of neighborhood dogs.

His sister, my aunt Camille, loved the pony club, dressing in an English-style riding habit complete with riding crop and helmet as she competed in jumping events. Dad, however, was a fantastic cowboy. He was Roy Rogers, or sometimes Zorro, riding his strawberry roan gelding Sandy. He and Sandy went everywhere—yards, trails, out on the road, around Oak Hill School—wherever he and Sandy wanted to go. There was a riding trail that started behind Robertson Academy and meandered to Leland Lane that everyone called the Bridle Path. After a long day on the trail, he would hitch Sandy to a long dog leash attached to a stake in his front yard. Sandy would graze a circular patch of grass like a lawn mower until it was time for him to go back to the barn.

In addition to Saturday trips to the farm with his father, arrangements were made for Sandy and my dad to visit Harlinsdale for a few weeks at a time in the summer and stay with his grandparents. His uncle Tom lived next door with his family, and Dad would ride all over the farm with his cousins, letting the smell and the beauty of it all work down into his soul. It was more than that, though. More than just beautiful fields and boyhood adventures. There was something about it that was alive.

The farm demanded something of the men who worked it, and they respected their responsibility to it. While he was playing at being a boy, there was something more important going on around him. Not that any of them would have said so, but he was starting to feel "in the way." He was starting to feel as though he were less than, not because of his size or his youth, but because he was just there to play while the men were there to work. Not anymore.

As the bus reached the city limits of Franklin, Dad stood and walked to the front to instruct the driver to stop at Harlinsdale Farm. Carrying his sack lunch, he stepped off the bus and headed down the long Lane to the Show Barn. By now everyone was already at work. His grandfather arrived later in the morning, as was his prerogative, so he decided to seek out his cousin Harlin Hayes, the farm manager, and formally ask for a job.

Vanus "Harlin" Hayes was the son of Dad's great-aunt Edna, his grandfather's sister. Harlin Hayes was therefore a cousin in his father's generation and at the time would have been nearly fifty-three, but he was Dad's cousin nonetheless. Harlin Hayes had developed a reputation as a fine horseman as a young man back in his twenties in Gamaliel[2], Kentucky, and in 1936 Wirt and Alex enticed him to move his young family to Franklin to help them establish Harlinsdale Farm. At six feet, four inches tall, he had earned the nickname "Hoss" back in Gamaliel. By the time Dad came along, no one called him anything except Mr. Hayes, or sir.

Mr. Hayes was a quiet man. That's not to say he didn't speak; he just didn't always use words when he communicated. Men watched Mr. Hayes to anticipate what he was trying to say without having to say it, hoping to do what he wanted without having to be asked. If he needed it done and you weren't doing it properly, he was liable to take over and do it himself, which

---

2 Named for a biblical figure in the book of Acts, properly pronounced *guh-may-lee-uhl*, but pronounced colloquially as *gah-mail-yah*.

was perhaps the worst rebuke he could give. He was a well-respected horseman, a man of impeccable character, and my dad was fearful and respectful of him.

Somehow Dad managed the words, "Mr. Hayes, sir, hi. My dad said to check with you about, well um, I was wanting… I'm here to work on the farm this summer. That is, I mean, I came to ask you for a job. Here. I want to work on the farm."

Mr. Hayes stared at him for what seemed like forever, until finally, a wide smile broke out across his face and he asked, "You do?"

"Yes, sir," Dad answered.

Mr. Hayes sized him up, squeezing his arm and making a show out of worrying over Dad's apparent lack of a bicep and finally answered, "Well, I guess we can find something for you to do."

Bloodlines

I only knew my great-grandfather when I was a small child, so you might say I only have picture memory of him. To differentiate him from my grandfather—who we called Granddaddy—me and my sisters called my great-grandfather Old-Old Granddaddy, and his wife Luella was appropriately called Old-Old Grandmother. I really hope they had a sense of humor about that, but in our defense, he was nearly a hundred years old at the time.

I knew my own grandfather rather well in his old age, and in those years he devoted nearly all of himself to Harlinsdale Farm and the Tennessee walking horse industry. In his middle age, however, he was conflicted. In those years he also enjoyed his life as a successful businessman and suburban father, complete with golf outings and country clubs, but his heart always pulled him back to his heritage.

His grandfather, Henry "Clay" Harlin[1], was a hardworking horseman and farmer from Gamaliel—seven generations and a few spelling variations removed from his ancestor George

---

1 Henry Clay Harlin was invariably called Clay. For the purposes of distinguishing him from his great-grandson—my father, Clayton "Clay" Harlin—Henry Clay be referred to in these stories by his first and middle name. I hope both he and the reader will forgive me.

Harland, who moved his family from Durham, England to the Pennsylvania colony in 1692. From Pennsylvania to Delaware, as far south as the Carolinas, and then following Daniel Boone's trail through the Cumberland Gap into Kentucky, the Harlands, Harlans, Harlings, and Harlins[2] developed a strong tradition of raising fine horses.

Alexander Harlin, Henry Clay's father, had eleven children. His first wife, Matilda, died when she was only thirty, but not before she bore five of them. One in particular, my great-great grandfather Clay's half-brother Lafayette Harlin, served in the Ninth Kentucky Infantry Regiment (U.S.) as a Captain during the Civil War. Alexander's second wife, Priscilla, had six more children, the youngest three being Henry Clay and his two sisters, Marietta and Martha, all of whom were born when Alexander was well into his forties. When it came marrying time they didn't have to look too far outside their hometown of Gamaliel because their neighbors Samuel and Elizabeth Comer happened to have one daughter and two sons of about the same age—Mary Bit, Samuel, and Leo. The Harlins and Comers celebrated three marriages together in the 1880s.

Henry Clay and Mary Bit had four children: daughters Edna and Florence and sons Alexander and William ("Wirt"). My family has a habit of reusing the same five or six names, and if there is still a living Harlin sharing your name, well then you are destined to be called by a variation of your first name, or as often as not, your middle name. The extended family being crowded with Williams and Wills and Bills at the time, my great-grandfather was forever known as Wirt. As evidenced by his own father Clay, Harlin Hayes, my dad's brother Wirt,

---

[2] All four spellings of this name are used in the Harland genealogy records, as well as handwritten entries made in the family bible which dates to the early 19th century and is still in our family's possession.

and in fact myself, the go-by-your-middle-name phenomenon is rampant in my family.

Wirt's mother, Mary Bit, died tragically from tuberculosis when he was not but two years old. She was four months shy of her twenty-seventh birthday. Wirt would never know his mother, and Henry Clay would never remarry. His own mother, Priscilla, was crippled and came to live with him and his children. She was stern, and life was not easy.

Wirt liked to tell his grandchildren that when he was a boy, his family didn't celebrate Christmas. Work around the farm never stopped, and even if they did manage to finish all their chores, Wirt and Alex would be sent down to the creek until the daylight expired to collect rocks to be used later as gravel. Wirt's escape from this life of hardship was horses.

Henry Clay Harlin established himself as a horseman, hiring out his expertise as a herdsman to local farmers when it came time to drive their cattle down to market in Carthage, Tennessee, on the Cumberland River. He had a natural way with horses and a reputation for raising some of the finest livestock in the area, and he passed this instinct down to his sons.

On Sundays, the only day when Wirt had a brief reprieve from his chores around the farm, he would put on the finest clothes he owned, saddle up one of his father's finest horses, and go out courting. By the time he was of age, Wirt had raised and sold few of his own horses, an investment that helped to fund his new start in life.

As soon as he was able, Wirt left Gamaliel and set out on his own. The details are not quite clear, but around this time his father sold the farm in Gamaliel and moved in with his daughter Edna and her new husband, Vanus Hayes. Wirt went to a business college in Bowling Green, Kentucky, that would later be the Western Kentucky University. After graduation he taught school for a year in New Jersey before moving to Nashville in 1909. He landed a job in a wholesale mercantile operation and was beginning to establish himself in the clothing manufacturing business when war broke out in Europe.

On June 5, 1917, Congress decreed that all unmarried men between the ages of twenty-one and thirty were "eligible and liable" for selective service in the U.S. military. Wirt was still unmarried at age thirty, and still six months shy of his thirty-first birthday, thus giving rise to the family legend that he was the oldest man drafted into the Army in World War I. Statistically speaking, I'm sure there was at least one other fellow older than him, but I've never cared to prove it so we're sticking by our claim. Wirt and his cousin Gus Comer would serve together stateside, being selected for promotion to sergeant and put to work corralling and training the new recruits who were by and large a decade younger.

After being released from military service, Wirt got busy living life. In 1922 he courted and married my great-grandmother, Luella Leek, and set to work establishing himself as a Tennessee businessman. Prior to his service in the Army, he began a venture in Nashville with his cousin, Claude Williams. In 1923 he was joined by his older brother Alex and together the three cousins established the Red Kap clothing manufacturing company. Initially making bib overalls and work clothes during the 1920s and '30s, they re-tooled their factories to make military uniforms and coveralls for the U.S. Army and Navy during the buildup to the Second World War. In less than one generation, he had taken his family's prospects from that creek bed in Gamaliel, Kentucky, to a new corporate office in Nashville's tallest skyscraper.

It is not lost on me that my great-grandfather prospered during the Great Depression while millions of Americans struggled. Had he stayed in Gamaliel and continued the life of a rural farmer and herdsman like his ancestors, subsistence and hardship would no doubt have defined his life. As the United States began a second industrial revolution and the rapid expansion of its military, the demand for textile manufacturers to produce work clothes for factory laborers and military uniforms—even canvas leggings, cartridge belts, and gas mask carriers—grew exponentially. Whether by chance or shrewd foresight, Wirt and Alex had made very sound investments of their energy and capital.

In 1932, Wirt's wife Luella gave birth to the couple's fourth child, all of whom were boys: William, Thomas, Alexander, and the newborn Robert. My great-grandfather was grateful for all that life had given him, but he knew most of what made him successful was rooted in the value of hard work he had learned as a boy in rural Kentucky.

Perhaps out of a self-conscious fear that someone might notice his habit of being impeccably dressed and mistake him for a city boy, he was fond of reminding people that he had worked too hard in his life to get out of his denim overalls to ever consider wearing them again. But while he may have earned the right to keep his hands clean, he still wanted his sons to know where they came from. He needed them to understand the blood of eight generations of American horsemen ran through their veins.

On summer afternoons and weekends, Wirt and Luella liked to take their boys to a place in Franklin called Willow Plunge, a privately-owned country club of sorts on the southeast side of town. The club featured two spring-fed swimming pools, tennis courts, a miniature golf course, and a sun-bathing area.

Located on the western edge of the Carnton Plantation, it was a popular spot for folks to escape the heat of a Tennessee summer during the Great Depression.

Wirt couldn't help but notice during these trips from his house in Nashville down to Franklin that many of the large estates in the area had fallen into receivership. He also had an eye for good farmland and knew the land between the limestone hills along Franklin Road down to the Harpeth River held rich Huntington soil that was ideal for growing hay and supporting livestock. So it was that in 1935, Wirt purchased the Myles Manor residence, and the adjacent acreage that became Harlinsdale Farm.

Twenty-nine years later, in the early summer of 1964, Wirt drove from his house down the Lane to the Show Barn late one morning, as was his custom. He was always well dressed in a finely tailored suit, complete with a hat and bow tie. As Dan Ford would say, "You could cut a piece of cheese with the crease in his pants." After taking in the sights and smells of his beautiful farm, he would settle into his chair in the office to the left of the marble entryway. Surrounded by portraits of the champion show horses that were bred and raised at Harlinsdale Farm, he'd light up a big cigar and reflect on where he'd come from.

His nephew, Harlin Hayes, came down to Franklin from Gamaliel in 1936 to entertain an offer from Wirt to be his farm manager. It was hard to believe at the time, but Wirt's dream came to life over the following decades due in large part to his nephew's leadership and hard work. They now managed hundreds of horses scattered over several farms in Williamson County. They had several champion stallions that produced highly-prized foals every year. They ran a herd of Hereford cattle and kept the next year's crop of yearling walking horse colts down on another property in Hillsboro, Tennessee, owned by the Harlins but managed by another Gamaliel transplant, Homer Ford.

Wirt's oldest son, William Wirt Harlin, Jr., who everyone now called Bill, had attended the U.S. Naval Academy in what would have been the class of 1948; but as the war wound down, he was released from the service and returned home to Franklin. You didn't get anything from Wirt Harlin unless you earned it, and so Wirt told his son Bill that if he wanted to work in the family business, be it at Harlinsdale or Red Kap, he was going to start at the bottom. By 1964, Bill had taken over as the chief financial officer at Red Kap and was branching out into the industrial laundry business. Like his father, Bill's heart was still on the farm. He had raised his children to know horses and would bring his son Clay down to the barn on Saturdays and for weeks at a time in the summer to stay with Wirt and Luella.

So, when Wirt heard his grandson's voice in the hallway of the Show Barn that summer morning, it didn't immediately catch him off guard. Maybe young Clay's mother Barbara had dropped him off to stay with his grandparents that week and Luella just hadn't told him yet. This was a welcome thought, and he knew little Clay's uncle Tom and his cousins John and Carter would be happy to have him around.

Expecting to see young Clay step out into the sunlit hallway of the Barn holding the reins of his little horse Sandy, Wirt instead saw his eleven-year-old grandson walking with a purpose out toward the Long Barn. Rather than a pony or a .22 plinking rifle, he was toting a pitchfork and manure scoop, trying as hard as his little legs would allow to keep up with the 6'4" Harlin Hayes as he marched off to find Mr. Irwin and put my dad to work.

Henry Clay Harlin, born September 24, 1855. Separated by death in 1889 from his only wife, Mary Bitt Comer, he was buried next to her on April 22, 1950.

Alexander Harlin (1812-1866) and Samuel Comer (1811-1877).

Henry Clay and his Children: Wirt, Alex, Florence, and Edna, c. 1910.

Wirt, Clay, and Alex, c. 1915.

Wirt Harlin, the last man drafted in World War I, earned his sergeant's stripes.

Wirt Harlin (5) and his cousin Gus Comer (1) during their service in the Army, c. 1918.

Grampa Clay, flanked by his grandsons Bill and Tom.
Their proud father Wirt looks on in the background, c. 1930.

Harlin Hayes and his wife Maurie with their daughter Mary Etta, c. 1937.

Standing left to right are Bill, Alex, and Tom.
Seated in Wirt's lap is Bob, c 1945.

Occupying the box of famed Harlinsdale Farm, Franklin, are from left: Tom Harlin, Mrs. W. W. Harlin Jr., W. W. Harlin Jr., and Mrs. Tom Harlin.

Tom and Bill attend the Celebration horse show with their wives, c. 1950.

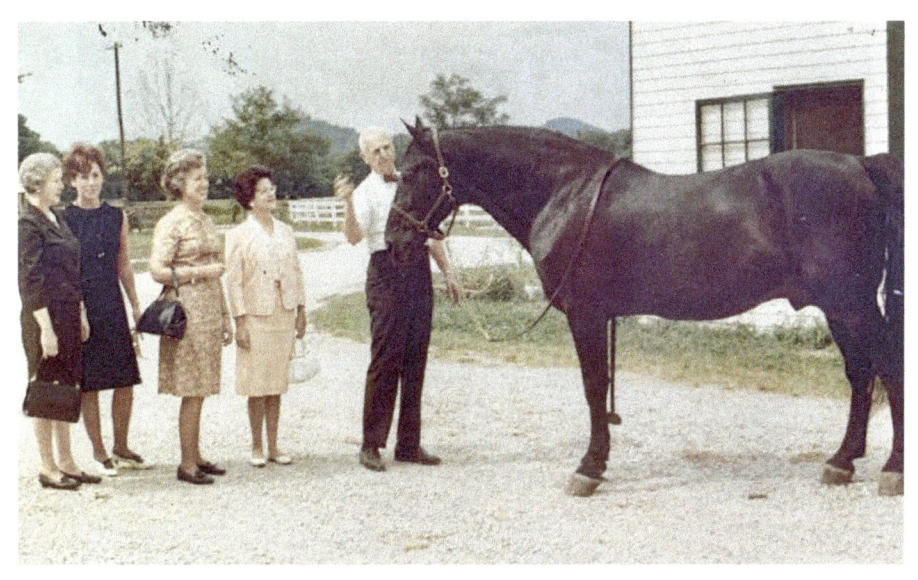

Wirt Harlin, the ladies' man, shows off Midnight Sun, c. 1960.

Wirt Harlin and his prized stallion Pride of Midnight, c. 1975.

Young Clay, his mother Barbara, brother Wirt, father Bill, and sister Camille, c. 1958

Camille, Wirt, and Clay (sporting a coonskin cap), c. 1956.

Bill and Clay Harlin, 1985.

Clay, Talbot, and Bill Harlin, 1985.

"OFF YOUR BUTTS AND ON YOUR FEET!

OUT OF THE SHADE AND IN THE HEAT!"

-CLAY HARLIN

(HARLINSDALE MOTIVATIONAL SPEECH)

Down to the Upper Barn

Anyone driving down Franklin Road on a June morning in the 1990s would've looked out on Harlinsdale Farm and seen acres upon acres of grazing horses. The large fields on either side of the Lane in the early summer would've had dozens of postpartum mares grazing while their young foals pranced around and played at being horses. The large field behind the main barns would've had another dozen or more with foals born earlier in the spring. Just north of that field in a square pasture bordering the Harpeth River would be last year's stock of yearling fillies, while their male counterparts worked out their newly testosterone-fueled egos in another field that ran as far south as the old Myles Manor property.

The description of landmarks, barns, and fields around Harlinsdale was not consistent. As best I can tell, the era in which the speaker was introduced to the farm tended to be the determining factor. In its early days, the property around Mr. Hayes' old house was the center of the farm, whereas in its final form this was only about the northernmost third of the property. One of the first barns built in the late '30s was the large barn on an adjacent hilltop to the Hayes house that my generation would have called Oscar's Barn. I wish I could tell you why we called it this, but I honestly don't know; perhaps because Oscar was primarily responsible for feeding it on the off days since he lived in one of the houses on the farm.

The next barn, which was already on the property at the time of purchase and probably dates back to the nineteenth century, was down to the southwest and lay lower on the hill toward the Harpeth River. That apparently made this the Lower Barn, so to my dad and his generation that made Oscar's Barn the Upper Barn. This was perplexing to me because I considered the Show Barn, which lay farther to the south, to be the center of the farm. If you were at the Show Barn and you needed to go to Oscar's Barn (or the Upper Barn), you would go "down the Lane." So to go down the Lane to the Upper Barn was illogical. As if this weren't enough, going "down the Lane" was actually a journey to the north and higher in elevation, which one might argue would be "up the Lane," geographically speaking.

The Long Barn, mercifully, was self-explanatory. It was a long, white, single story horse stable with about ten stalls on either side and lay just to the northwest of the Show Barn.

Southwest of the Show Barn originally sat a concrete slab and some brick sheds that held coal for the old railroad and power plant. The Colt Barn was built on this foundation around the time I started working at Harlinsdale, its original purpose being to house the expanding herd of yearling colts we produced each year, thus the name. At least that's what I called it. It is entirely possible that my dad and the older guys were actually saying Coal Barn, in reference to its original purpose of storing coal, but to my ears Colt Barn made sense. At this point I actually enjoy the fact that it's still a mystery and would rather not know the truth. To make matters worse, before my time there was a hot walker—something used to cool down horses after exercise—installed on this foundation and some of the older hands would also call it the Walker Barn.

The Breeding Barn, sometimes in old stories called the Breeding Shed, and just as often the Stud Barn, lay further to the southwest of the Colt Barn and just east of the Back Lane.

The Tractor Barn[1] lay to the south of the Show Barn and, as its name suggests, served as a tractor garage and workshop in addition to storing the dry wood shavings used for bedding. Because this building also housed the large silo of grain that we fed to the horses, it was just as often referred to as the Granary, although I don't believe I ever once called it that.

These four barns—the Long Barn, Colt Barn, Breeding Barn, and Tractor Barn—along with the Show Barn, would collectively be described as the Main Barns.

If right now you're just a little confused, then I think I can thoroughly finish the job. The Lane was uniformly agreed to be the main paved entrance that ran from Franklin Road west to the Show Barn. This pavement ended in a roundabout that circumnavigated the Show Barn and turned to gravel about halfway around its circumference. This gravel road continued west past the Colt Barn and the Long Barn until it ended at a T intersection with a different gravel road. Herein lies the problem. It was common to be sent down this other gravel road to complete some task or another, but for some reason that only made sense at Harlinsdale, we also called this other road the Lane.

I guess if pressed on the matter we would have called it the Back Lane as alluded to earlier, but no one ever really said that. It was all in the context. The Back Lane, if we're calling it that, was a much longer north-south gravel road that ran the

---

[1] The Tractor Barn originally housed the coal-fired power plant that generated electricity for the railway.

entire length of the rectangular property and roughly followed the road bed of the old interurban railway that ran all the way to Nashville[2]. Saying someone was *coming* down the Lane meant they had turned off Franklin Road and were heading toward the Show Barn:

"Y'all seen Mr. Harlin yet this morning?"

"Seen him comin' down the Lane just now."

Telling someone to "Go down the Lane" meant to head north, down to the Upper Barn:

"Oscar, go on down the Lane with these boys and clean out those sheds in that old barn up there."

Down the Lane (technically up) and in three separate but connected fields were the mares. This was a herd of a hundred or so female Tennessee walkers—some owned by Harlinsdale, while most were boarded on the farm in expectation of breeding with one of our stud horses and leaving later in the summer "in foal." Individually, as with all horses, they had their own unique personalities. As a herd they became a feral mass that resembled the Brumby Mob in *The Man From Snowy River*. If you haven't seen that film then you should go watch it right now and come back when you are finished.

Inside the Show Barn, specifically on the south side, were the stud horses. World champions like Pride's Gold Coin, Pride's Genius, Pride's Dark Spirit, Motown Magic, and Dark Spirit's Rebel, to name a few. The remaining stalls in the Show

---

[2] In the farm's early days, Homer Ford recalled tearing up the old track along with each and every railroad tie that lined this road.

Barn housed various mares boarded for breeding, usually ones that needed special medical or dietary attention during their stay.

Another twenty or so stalls in the Long Barn and another dozen in the Colt Barn would be home to various mares whose owners had paid for the stall boarding option and were waiting to be in season for breeding. Later in the summer as the breeding season wound down, the new crop of yearlings would move into these stalls to begin their training. Down (up) the Lane in Oscar's Barn would be the last few mares who had yet to foal that year. This barn had swinging dividers between some of the stalls that allowed them to be opened to provide more space for a momma and baby. The newest of the new babies could be seen trying out their long new legs in the small pastures around the barn.

Now, a casual observer might drive by the farm on that June morning and think we spent our days in the saddle riding those fields on horseback, but nothing could be further from the truth. This was a breeding farm. In addition to the care and feeding of all these animals, the bulk of the daily routine in June and early July centered around the breeding schedule. Now don't get me wrong, I did get to ride. Before I realized how much easier—and safer—it was to collect the Brumby Mob using a tractor, I would saddle up one of the geldings and go round them up on horseback. My preferred mount was a palomino named Trigger.

I'm sure it amused everyone, possibly annoyed them, that I took this job unto myself, thus absolving me of some stall cleaning duty, but it was fun. My motivation for this approach waned as the summer went on, however. There were a few outlaw bands amongst the Brumby Mob who didn't have much respect for me or Trigger. After getting kicked in the shins a few times and being along for the ride as Trigger wheeled and fought back with teeth and hooves, I also opted for the tractor approach. We never had a four-wheeler or a UTV on the farm. Apparently the four-wheeler was to my grandfather what the tractor was to an earlier generation—an abominable eye sore that marked the end of a more glorious and morally superior era of farm work.

Once I had taken Trigger from this stall in the Show Barn, ridden down (up) the Lane to round up the mares from the Back Field, then herded them back down past Oscar's Barn and the Lower Barn, driven them all the way back down the Lane, across the old railroad bridge and behind the Long Barn, through the gate that separated the Lane from the Lane, then past the Walker Barn and out into the paddock behind the Breeding Shed, my journey into this strange new world was only just beginning.

Country Horsemanship

Breeding days seem to dominate my memory of the early summer, but truthfully it was only Mondays, Wednesdays, Fridays, and cleanup on Saturday mornings. Tuesdays and Thursdays were maintenance days of some sort or another. But on a breeding day, sometime between halfway through throwing out the Long Barn in the morning and before Monty[1] showed up, Dad and Rocky would begin prepping the battlefield.

Scores of data that I don't pretend to understand and was never privy to—and most of which was kept inside their heads—drove the workload each day. Which mares were close to ovulating, which mares had been bred earlier that week or last and might need another round, which mares had been bred weeks before and needed to be checked by Monty for being in foal, how many mares per stud factoring in how much each stud averaged per collection (oh yes, there will be a story about this part; don't worry), which mares teased accurately, and which ones would try and take the teasing stud's head off no matter how in heat they really were.

---

1 Dr. Monty McInturff, DVM. He took over as the primary veterinarian for Harlinsdale after Dr. Johnny Haffner, who took over after Dr. DeWitt Owen. Monty is a staunch supporter and fundraiser for the Friends of Franklin Parks, the organization that preserves Harlinsdale in its current form as a city park.

I could never pretend to know these things; I just rounded the horses up from the field and went back to throwing out stalls. Dad and Rocky, however, could look at this swarming herd of mares, each vying to get to the farthest corner of the catch pen, and at a glance call out her name, lineage, owner, and the current state of her ovulation cycle. This was a rodeo I was able to participate in as I got older and bigger, or maybe just more experienced as a horseman, but trying to catch "that bay mare with the 9 white tag" out of this mob could be pretty dangerous. Confidence went a long way; timidity would get you hurt.

Based on Rocky's clairvoyant powers with regard to the equine estrous cycle, some of the mares we cut from the herd would pass straight through to await Monty's ultrasound machine, but most would be put through a more natural test first—the teasing stud. This was a very specialized profession that required a very specific type of stud horse. In this case it was Dee-Bo. I have no idea what his pedigree name was, where he came from, or how he found himself in this occupation. He was a big sway-backed, barrel-chested, jet black stallion. He had a thick black mane with a shiny lock of hair that fell over one eye, like a villain in a James Bond movie. Or more appropriate to his job, like some sort of equine adult movie star from the '70s.

Dee-Bo was a perfect teasing stud because, while he had all the instincts of a breeding stallion, he seemed to lack any motivation to consummate the act. He also seemed to be immune to either rejection or desire on the part of his prospective mate. In short, Dee-Bo was great at his job because he just didn't really care. He could give a mare all the signals of a stud horse looking for love and then go right back to scratching his rear end on a fence post. Other studs would tear down the barn, trying to get to a mare in heat, but Dee-Bo would have to be roused out of catnaps between mares to get back to work.

Eventually the mares selected to be checked by Monty would be cut out and tied up around a square corral outside the breeding barn. One by one they would be brought into this stockade contraption capable of holding three horses side by side with locking gates at the front and back. The back gate was low enough to block any attempts to kick out while granting access to the business end of a broodmare. Her tail would be secured up and out of the way, rear end washed with surgical soap and warm water. Monty would palpate them manually or examine them with an ultrasound machine to determine if they were already in foal, had ovulated recently, or were imminently about to do so.

The mares were brought in according to the schedule determined by Rocky and Dad, orders being delivered by shout from inside the breeding room. This room was a smallish twelve-foot by twelve-foot chemistry lab of sorts, outfitted with all the paraphernalia of semen collection and artificial insemination, as well as stainless steel counters and deep sinks, a refrigerator/freezer, microscope, and a hemacytometer capable of determining the number of live sperm cells per CC of volume. That final machine would determine the number of mares capable of being bred that day based on size of the collection and odds of achieving success, based in large part on Monty's ovary check.

Not all farm work is equally enjoyable; each job comes with its pros and cons. Being on mare-catching duty relieved one of the hard labor of picking up manure piles, but also robbed you of the camaraderie found on that work detail, not to mention the occasional chance to drive the tractor and operate the manure spreader. Catching mares for the breeding day also exposed you to more of the illogical language used by the old hands at Harlinsdale.

Orders delivered from the breeding room sounded something like:

"Get that bay mare, 19 red."

Translation: Bring in the dark red mare, black markings, with a collar around her neck, holding a red tag and the number 19; easy.

"Talbot, go get that black mare, down a ways from that colt with the neck drain."

Translation: "Colt with the neck drain" indicated something in the Show Barn, probably pretty obvious if one were to glance into the stalls, looking for a colt with a plastic tube sticking out of its neck. "Down a ways" indicated more than one stall, but probably not all the way to the end. Best case scenario: seventy-five percent chance of success on the first try.

The disparity that exists between country horsemanship and classical horsemanship deserves more unpacking, but for the sake of this story it is important to understand that the words chosen to describe a horse could vary from person to person, and may not have continuity throughout the day, even coming from the same person. For instance, the words *chestnut* and *sorrel* could be interchangeable to describe a light, reddish-brown horse with a mane and tail of the same or perhaps lighter brown color. *Roan* was interchangeable with the much more country appropriate *blue*, and sometimes to my amateur eye was used to describe horses that were really a more dapple gray.

A *bay* is a horse with dark reddish hair and a black mane and tail, usually devoid of any white markings, save maybe a star or stripe in the forehead. Sometimes a black mare could take on the look of a bay if she were out in the sun and her coat had become reddish at a glance, but would still be described as black.

Often a more obvious physical trait would trump coat color and a horse may just be described by a large white blaze on their face, or the presence of warts on their muzzle, or even just their obvious personality traits: "…that mean old heifer, next to that blaze-face mare with the warts." The absence of cows altogether meant the word *heifer* in this case was being used as a euphemism for an ornery mare.

Not that titles meant anything at Harlinsdale, but Dad was technically the farm manager and Rocky was technically the stallion manager, which meant he oversaw the farm's breeding program. Rocky was a genius savant when it came to horses. He knew them all by sight and kept every detail about them in his head. He could see the one mare he needed out of a swirling pack of brood mares and call her out by name. He worked from a clipboard during the breeding day, but I got the impression this was more or less a prop. Rocky was also a man of few words, especially when he was juggling all this data in his head during a breeding day, so you had to be quick on the uptake and pay attention when he gave orders.

All things considered, I would no sooner ruin the surprise of this fantastic new world than I would spoil the adventures of Narnia that awaited young Lucy on the other side of the wardrobe. The strange new language, the illogical and obtuse way people would tell you to do something without giving you any of the requisite details about how to do it. Three names for each barn, three different ways to describe the same horse, north was down, lower was higher, and "the back" of some field or even the entire property could be any number of different directions. I guess they could have made it easy, or at least given some consideration to a newcomer who was understandably lost for a few days, but easy was one word you'd never hear anyone use to describe anything at Harlinsdale Farm.

That Yella Mare with the Red Tag

So there I was, standing outside the breeding room, waiting for my next set of orders. For some reason, Rocky was in a foul mood this day and I don't pretend to know why. Something above my pay grade must not have been going well and all I heard was,

"Get that yella mare with the red tag!"

Now this violated several elements of the system. For one thing, there were "tags" and there were "neck tags." The former was a triangle-shaped, color-coded, and numbered tag that hung at the end of a stiff white rope around the mare's neck; the latter was a colored plastic strap that was about an inch wide with the number on the side. In either case there were bound to be more than one red "tag" or red "neck tag" and I was going to need to know the number. But fine; give him the benefit of the doubt. Maybe there was only one "yella" mare out there with a red tag, making the number irrelevant and so that should narrow it down.

"Yella," in this case, was used in place of the more formal "palomino" to describe a light brown horse with a blonde mane and tail, not a commonly occurring color for walking horses. The problem here is that there was only one yella mare on the entire farm and she was out in one of the back fields with her new foal—definitely not tied up in the corral. Incidentally, she was Trigger's momma, making Trigger the only other palomino horse on the property, but he was of course a gelding and certainly not up next for an ovary check. The one thing I knew for sure was that asking for clarification would only make things worse and potentially relegate me back to stall-cleaning duty, so I decided to tromp out into the paddock and take my chances.

What I found outside was the usual assortment of Bays, Blacks, and Sorrels with all the available combinations of colored neck tags and collars. The only thing left to do was to find the lightest of all the chestnut mares out there with a red tag and give it a shot, chestnut being the closest thing I could see to "yella." This probably narrowed it down to two or three, and of course I chose wrong.

Now it's not like you could walk back into the breeding barn, toting a mare and ask, "Is this the one?" and get an answer. There were too many other things going on at the same time and Rocky had already moved on in his mind, likely assuming I had my job covered. The only thing to do was hope and then go ahead and secure her in the stockade and wait. I didn't have to wait too long for a judgment as Monty moved over to check my mare and asked,

"What's the story with this one, Rocky?"

Without responding to Monty directly, without even glancing up from his clipboard, Rocky said,

"Naw, uh-uh. Go get that yella mare out there, on the back fence."

Ok; that cleared up exactly nothing. The fact that Rocky knew precisely where this mare was tied up, was standing in the breezeway of the barn with a clear view of the corral, capable of pointing straight at the mare he was talking about—but instead chose to further obfuscate the situation—was not lost on me. Back out to the corral I went, toting my poor, confused, light chestnut mare with a red tag out to the fence to tie her up and try again.

"Back Fence" was by no means an agreed-upon description of anything specific as far as I was aware. Eliminating all the other possible fences on the entire farm, and isolating my search specifically to the corral outside the breeding room, there were two sides of the square fence that could each be considered the "back," depending on how you entered the corral. Considering Rocky's point of view, generally seeing the corral from the breeding room, I decided on the northernmost side farthest from the barn.

Things were finally starting to turn in my favor, as there was only one chestnut mare (which, at this point, I had just given up reconciling why he was saying *yella* instead of *chestnut*) and she did indeed have a red neck tag, albeit the wider plastic collar version and not the hanging tag. Under normal circumstances I would have scrutinized this distinction, but now decided to just let it go. To the stockade we went, her tail tied up and out of the way, rear end properly washed off and waiting for the vet check. Wrong again.

From the breeding room I heard,

"Naw, uh-uh. We dun got that one already."

Someone with a little more assertiveness than a fifteen-year-old boy might have given Rocky the business over his piss-poor communication skills, not to mention his sour attitude. I did know enough from growing up around country people that this would only make things worse. Fifteen years later I would be flying F-18s from an aircraft carrier and doing close air support missions in Afghanistan, and without realizing it I somehow tapped into this future skill set. That is, if trying to talk someone onto a target when their vantage point is drastically different from yours, begin by talking about something large and obvious until you find common ground. Find something you can both agree on and then work big to small until you gain a positive identification of your target. Most important: find something unique about your target that eliminates the chance of mistaken identity.

"Okay, Rocky," I said, "I see a few chestnut mares out there. The only light-colored ones with red tags are the two I brought in. But there are some other chestnut mares out there with red tags, so what's the number on the tag of the one you're looking for?"

Rocky, finally realizing we were speaking different languages, took a last drag on his cigarette while eyeing me quizzically. Clipboard in one hand, he stomped over to the entrance to the barn, planted his feet, and squared up to his target.

"Are you lookin'?!" he asked as he glanced over his shoulder at me while twisting the toe of his boot into the ash of the Marlboro Red he had just flicked to the ground. "Right there."

At about ten feet on a direct line from the end of his outstretched finger was a yellow mare, wearing a red, numberless tag, tied up to the fence on the back of the corral.

Now, in my defense, this mare had done a fair bit of rolling in the mud. Her mud-stained tail was darker than her light brown coat, giving her a chestnut color from the rear end. She was also tied up outside the corral on the east side toward the Show Barn. To me, this was definitely the front fence if there ever was one. But as Rocky saw it, from the direction he would have entered the corral from the catch pen to tie up a mare, she was "on the back fence." I might have corrected him and said "on the back *of* the fence," but at this point it was too late.

She also had no number on her red tag. For some unknown reason, when she was dropped off they affixed this tag on her before realizing it was a numberless factory defect, but then decided to just leave her as "no number" red tag. After all, she was only one of two palomino mares on the entire farm; how hard could it be to keep up with her?

Finally seeing things for the first time, I realized "yella mare with the red tag on the back fence" was a perfectly reasonable description of this horse. I had failed to pay attention to Rocky's logic, beautiful in its simplicity. All three of his descriptors were unique to this particular mare, but I wrongly assumed he had made some sort of oversight by not giving me the number on her tag. In his own purposefully obtuse way, something he probably learned from Mr. Hayes, he had actually given it to me—by omitting it altogether.

I grudgingly stomped out of the barn to retrieve my prize, and just as I approached her to untie the lead line, she stomped a big, impatient hoof into a mud puddle under the fence line as if to say, "bout time you figured that out." I turned over in my mind just what I would say to defend myself when I got back to the barn. I could not have been the only person present who realized just how ridiculous and frustrating that entire episode had been.

Indignant and freshly speckled with mud from head to toe, I pulled the rope to release the safety knot that held the "yella mare with the red tag tied to the back fence." Just then I heard over my shoulder, "After that one, go get that big-headed mare in the Show Barn."

The Show Barn of Harlinsdale Farm.

Aerial view of Harlinsdale c. 1965, Show Barn in center. Behind and to the right is the Long Barn. To the left is the Tractor Barn, and behind that is the Breeding Barn. Just to the right of the Breeding Barn are the coal sheds that became the Colt Barn.

WHERE THE GREAT ONES GATHER.

At Harlinsdale Farm, we place quite a lot of importance on the outstanding performance records of our stallions, because we know performance is one of the single most important criteria in selecting a stallion for your farm's breeding program.

But we both know it takes much more than an outstanding show ring record to produce the type of foal we all want to produce.

That's why, in addition to great show records, we've also worked hard to bring you the best bloodlines the Tennessee Walking Horse world has to offer . . .

And why we've invested over a half century perfecting the crosses which will produce champions for you.

Harlinsdale Farm

An advertisement featuring the marble entryway of the Show Barn looking out to the east, the direction from which you might see someone "coming down the lane".

The interior of the Show Barn looking north.

A view inside the Show Barn looking through the entryway to the west.

Aerial View of Harlinsdale c. 1945 looking northwest.
1—Myles Manor, 2—Show Barn, 3—Tractor Barn, 4—Breeding Barn
5—Lower Barn, 6—Upper Barn, 7—Hayes House
Note—the Long Barn, and Colt barn had not yet been built.

The notorious Church Pew.

Clay Harlin showing off a yearling in front of the Long Barn, c. 1965

The Colt Barn center, Breeding Barn to the left.

The Breeding Barn.

The Harlinsdale crew in front of the Hayes House, c. 1950.

Alfred in action with the round bailer, c. 1990.
Lower Barn (with silo) in the foreground and the Upper Barn in the background.

A mare and foal in the field just north of the Long Barn.
Behind them is one of the several fields that made up the Back Field.

Clay Harlin parks out a yearling colt in front of the Upper Barn, c. 1980.
Lower Barn (with silo) visible in the background.

The Mares—A herd of female brood mares who inhabited the Back Field and had to be rounded up on breeding days. The *go ahead and try it* look on the mare in the foreground was typical of this lot.

The Show Barn in 2004, at the time of the farm's sale to the city of Franklin.

Looking north, down the "Back" Lane towards the Upper barn.

The south end of the Show Barn, Tractor Barn to the right, 2004.

The Upper Barn, 2004.

"He's about as lost as last year's Easter egg."

-Dan Ford

Syrup Lips, alias Dynamic Dan

There are a few characters that loom large in my mind from those days. Most of them have passed on, some in the biblical sense and others in the sense that they've simply moved on in life and lost touch with us. Mr. Hayes died a year before I was born, but my great-grandfather died in 1986 at the age of ninety-nine; I was five. His son, my grandfather, passed on in 2017 at age ninety-two. Rocky Jones passed away in 2019 at the age of sixty-four, but some of us are still around—even if we seem to only get together anymore at funerals.

My dad, luckily, is still a conduit for me to peer back into this world as he maintains a healthy friendship with some of the men who were more prominent in his life. Johnny Haffner and Dan Ford are two who immediately come to mind, not only because of their importance to the story of Harlinsdale, but also in my memory as men who were larger than life. Good-ole, God-fearing, salt of the earth, hardworking men.

I don't think I ever saw Dan Ford when a smile didn't break out on his face before he spoke. He used to be able to roll his stomach like someone was driving a rolling pin across it over and over in waves. He'd pull this trick while you were trying to have a serious conversation with someone, with him standing just behind them but where only you could see. For most of his adult life he was an over-the-road truck driver[1] and he used to amuse us with stories of chiming in on CB radio conversations using a handle like "Syrup Lips" or "Dynamic Dan." I have it on good authority that he christened old Mr. Irwin with the name "Puss[2]," and I know I heard him call different people "Moose Jaw," "Hoss," or "Cuz." I used to try and figure out his system for giving people nicknames, but I'm pretty sure these were just ubiquitous with Dan.

Dan's history with Harlinsdale goes back even before he was born, but he wasn't working full time at the farm during the summers I was there, except during the annual yearling auction when all the old hands showed up to help. Even still, he'd been a part of our life for as long as I could remember and he seemed to always be around.

Dan would drop in during the summer to visit every other week or so, and it was just about the only time you'd see everyone stop working for a while and just smile and laugh while they all talked. Once Dan realized he was holding up the show he'd grab a lunge line and take the next colt in line and work a few with us just so he could stay there and catch up with everyone. Appropriately, Dan was even there at the very end. In 2020, at the age of seventy-one, he climbed up in the hay loft with Dad and me to help us clean out every last hay bale from the loft of old the barn in College Grove before this final remnant of Harlinsdale was sold and gone forever.

Johnny Haffner was another character of my childhood and a lifelong friend of Harlinsdale. Johnny lived across the street from the farm in a house two doors down from the Factory. In 1972 at the age of fifteen, he walked across

---

[1] Dan drove for Yellow Freight for thirty three years, logging over 3 million miles without a single accident.
[2] Dan claims it was actually his grandfather Homer who first used this nickname for Mr. Irwin.

Franklin Road from his house and took the gravel drive that led to Mr. Hayes' house and knocked on the door. When Mr. Hayes answered, Johnny introduced himself and asked for a summer job. Johnny was enrolled at Battle Ground Academy about two years behind Dad, and he knew Mr. Hayes and my great-grandfather from going to church with them at Fourth Avenue Church of Christ. Mr. Hayes sized him up and asked him if he'd ever "worked with horses." Johnny was honest and admitted he'd played with a few horses but wasn't sure if he'd ever worked with one. Mr. Hayes must have appreciated his honesty more than his sense of humor and gave him a job.

Johnny worked at the farm with Dad and Rocky while they were all in high school and then attended the University of Tennessee, graduating from its nascent veterinary program. He started his own equine practice in Spring Hill, TN and eventually took over as the primary vet for Harlinsdale between 1982 and 1992. Like it was for all of us, those years at Harlinsdale were a very important part of his life and the relationships he formed and the memories they made are an important part of his life story. His friendship and steadfastness as a Christian brother and friend have been a rock my father could lean on throughout his life's trials.

I have shed some if not most of my Tennessee accent over the years, but I find it returns subconsciously in conversation whenever I try to say something with an air of wisdom. The way these men talked was an art form in itself, something I would try to adopt anytime I wanted to sound as though I had been there and seen a few things. I don't want anyone to think my attempt to preserve the colloquial way in which these stories were told to me is by any means meant to poke fun at the characters. These men were and are giants to me, full of wisdom and practical intelligence that I have rarely found anywhere else.

Johnny and Cathy Haffner, Clay and Faye Harlin, Linda and Dan Ford.
April 13, 2023, on the occasion of Clay's 70th birthday.

Tougher 'n Tarzan

In 1961, a thirteen-year-old Dan Ford headed out to the hayfield to help his granddaddy and the rest of the Harlinsdale boys get up a load of hay. He'd been driving his granddaddy's 1949 Ford pickup since he was about six, so getting to drive it out to the field that day was nothing remarkable. He wasn't quite big enough yet to hold his own on the hay wagon, but he could use his granddaddy's truck to ferry the unloaded wagons back from the barn and walk beside the wagons to pick up the occasional fallen bales.

Dan had been doing most things around the farm since he was a young boy, but this was the first summer where he was employed full time. His weekly wage was eighteen dollars for six days of work, but that didn't include the hours before and after his time at the farm in Franklin where he would help feed the horses and cows out in Hillsboro on another farm, owned by the Harlins, but managed by his grandfather, Homer Ford.

Homer and his wife Annie lived in the main house up on the hill, and Dan's parents Clark and Ruth raised him in the two-room log cabin "not big enough to cuss a cat in" that sat down in a muddy hollow—or holler, if you prefer—further back into the Hillsboro property. Dan's parents eventually moved him and his family to Nashville, but in the summers he always went back to live with Homer and Annie, who everyone called Daddy Ford and Momma Ford, on the farm that everyone just called Mr. Ford's place.

The Fords were there at the beginning, back even as far as Gamaliel, Kentucky. Dan's grandfather, Homer, was born in 1896 and moved to middle Tennessee looking for work around 1935, just as Wirt and his brother Alex were building up their farming enterprise. Homer originally settled on a piece of farmland out on Lewisburg Pike that Dan says his daddy, Clark Ford, called the Katydid Farm. The exact location of this farm is still somewhat of a mystery.

"Trying to get directions out of Daddy was like pulling teeth," according to Dan. "I'd ask Daddy, 'where was that Katydid Farm?' and he'd say 'Ahhh, you know it was a ways on down yonder.'"

Trying to get exact dates out of Harlinsdale's records is apparently also like pulling teeth, because as best we can tell, sometime in the forties, Harlinsdale acquired access to another farm out on Hillsboro Road in an area known as Leipers Fork. It is unclear whether Homer and Harlin Hayes knew each other back in Gamaliel, but in any event his reputation as a horseman and hardworking farmer recommended him for the job. Homer and his wife Annie moved into the main house on that property and became its overseer sometime before Dan was born in 1948. Dad has records of its purchase dated in the early fifties, but given that Dan was born in 1948 and his parents must have met out in Leiper's Fork in the mid-forties, it is reasonable to assume that Homer and Annie, along with their children, moved out to the farm that people began to refer to as the Hillsboro Farm, and then eventually as Mr. Ford's Place sometime around 1946.

Dan didn't live in a house with a bathroom in it until he was fifteen, when his family moved to Nashville. In the summer of 1961 they were still living in a small farmhouse in Leipers Fork whose bathroom facilities consisted of an outhouse. The cabin on the farm in Hillsboro where he spent his first seven years of life had no running water at all. By the time the Fords moved in, someone had run electricity to the cabin, but it was still not much more than a roof over their heads and a wood-burning stove to keep warm in the winter. More than anything, Dan remembers the herd of cows that seemed to always congregate around the front porch, keeping the mud about knee deep to a six-year-old boy.

Built sometime in the 1800s, the cabin's original occupants bore holes into the log walls to be used as firing ports in the likely event of a hostile raid by the area's natives or lawless bandits. This cabin sat right on the old Natchez Trace, an eighteenth-century overland trading route that linked the southernmost point of the Cumberland River just west of Nashville, to the eastern bend in the Mississippi River, just south of Natchez.

If you've ever spent even five minutes around Dan, you can't help but sense the positivity and humor with which he approaches life. Lack of modern comforts aside, even those available to most Americans in the 1950s, Dan's young life must have come with a healthy dose of love and gratitude that formed the basic building blocks for happiness.

Homer Ford, as only Dan can say, was "tougher n' Tarzan." Built from the same nineteenth-century Kentucky stock as Wirt Harlin and forged in the same fire that gave men like Harlin Hayes their steel backbone, Homer worked those two hundred acres in Hillsboro mostly by himself after his son Clark moved his family out of the log cabin in 1955. By the time Dan and his cousin Ben Bowman grew old enough to help, Homer was already into his sixties. Tractors were scarce on country farms in the 1930s and '40s, and in any event Homer would have preferred mule power.

He would mow the pastures on that farm with a ground-powered mower pulled by his team of mules, Joe and Ed. Some of the hills were so steep that Dan can remember seeing his granddaddy hanging off the side of the mower so far, he might as well have been riding it sideways.

To feed all the cows and horses kept out there during the winter, Homer would hitch one of his mules to the back of a hay wagon and pull it backward into the hay silo, and then load the wagon with nothing but a pitchfork. Homer would do this every day—twice a day—and that was before and after he went to Franklin to find whatever work was waiting for him at Harlinsdale.

Homer was a kind and patient man, and most of the boys who worked at Harlinsdale loved being sent out to "Mr. Ford's" for the day to catch colts or herd cows because they knew Daddy Ford loved being around young folks, and Momma Ford would feed them well. My own father remembers Homer as "one of the most gentle people I ever met in my life," a sentiment that Dan would agree with, save only once.

Dan was about six years old and still living in the old log cabin on the farm. His daddy Clark was off at work somewhere and his mother went to get Homer to tell him that his grandson wouldn't go to school. Dan had come down with some sort of polio-like affliction and said he couldn't walk. As luck would have it, Homer had just the right medicine and it turned out Dan could walk after all, but not before his granddaddy whipped him all the way across the yard and into the truck to take him to school.

Dan wasn't the kind of kid who had to learn a lesson more than once, and he never tried anything like that again. By the summer of 1961, he was getting into his teenage years and was starting to become aware of just how hard his granddaddy worked, of how hard they all worked. He wasn't going to give him any more trouble and he had resolved to do whatever he could to help out. He wished his granddaddy would just take a break in the truck for a while and let Dan get up on the wagon and help load hay, but that was not in Homer's DNA. Before Dan could even roll to a stop, Homer was already out the passenger-side door and walking to intercept the tractor, baler, and hay wagon train that Mr. Irwin was pulling across the hayfield.

Dan's older cousin Ben Bowman was on the other side of the field on another tractor raking hay and Dave Parish was up on the wagon by himself, trying not to get swamped by the hay bales coming up the chute from the hay baler. Dave already had the wagon about half loaded, which in and of itself was remarkable because he was also in his sixties, but it was clear he could use some help. This particular baler had its own Wisconsin engine mounted on the front instead of a power take-off shaft direct from the tractor. This two-cylinder gas engine had no exhaust muffler and was running wide open, like an outlaw Harley Davidson at full throttle.

Behind the baler was attached a hay wagon, probably one of the very same wagons I would stand on thirty-five years later. Mr. Irwin was pulling the whole train with a McCormick W-9 tractor that also lacked any sound suppression on its exhaust. Needless to say, voice communication was difficult and Mr. Irwin had to keep his eyes focused long down the rows of cut hay to stay lined up, rarely looking behind him when he was driving the tractor.

Dan watched his granddaddy approach the tongue of the tractor, a large round metal bar that attached it to the back end of the baler, and without even breaking stride he planted one foot on it, anticipating it as a step stool to get up on the moving wagon.

On the first attempt, Homer's foot slipped, and without a second thought he tried again, except now the front edge of the wagon was a good deal closer. To Dan's horror, Homer's foot slipped again, but this time he fell to the ground, the front edge of the wagon knocking him flat on his back. As if it were happening in slow motion, Dan watched the front wheel of the hay wagon roll right over Homer Ford's chest.

In the blink of an eye, Dan's granddaddy went from being the strong and indestructible hero of his youth, to a helpless old man crushed beneath a silly hay wagon. *Well that was it for Homer Ford*, they'd all say. They all knew the old man would work himself to death one day. He was too old to be out here trying to keep up with the young folks, but he just wouldn't quit. That went for Dave Parrish too; what were these two old timers trying to prove? Dan cursed himself. That should have been him and Ben up on that wagon, with Dave out raking hay on the tractor and Daddy Ford kicked back in the shade sitting in the cab of his truck.

How would he ever hold his head up, knowing his granddaddy took what should have been his place on the hay wagon that day? Why didn't they all stop him years ago? He didn't need to be out here anymore. There was plenty of other work he could do around the farm that wasn't so dangerous for an old man. Dan felt sick at the thought of seeing his grandmother and having to tell her what happened.

All this flashed through Dan's head in an instant as he bolted for the wagon, screaming for Mr. Irwin to stop. Dave

Parish was yelling too from atop the hay wagon, waving his arms frantically, but Mr. Irwin couldn't hear or see them. They had mere seconds before the mortally wounded Homer Ford got the coup de gras from the rear wheel of the hay wagon bearing down on him. Dan couldn't believe he'd have to watch helplessly as the wagon rolled over his granddaddy a second time.

Just then, as the rear wheel cast its shadow over him, Homer reached up with one arm and then the other, grabbed the side of the hay wagon, and hauled himself up off the ground. He hung there suspended, his legs still dragging on the ground, and the rear wheel turning against his side so close that it left skid marks on his shirt. Homer was stuck in this position, hugging the side of the wagon while Dan and Dave Parish yelled frantically at Mr. Irwin to halt the train. Ben, driving the other tractor, finally got Al's attention by tearing out across the field in front of his path to stop him.

With good, dry hay, a standard bale spit out the back of a New Holland square baler weighs about forty pounds. Ballpark numbers, let's say a good crew could stack a hundred bales on a wagon. This wagon then, which probably weighed about a thousand pounds empty, also carried about two thousand pounds of hay— half full, as Dan remembers it. So it isn't an exaggeration to say the man had about three thousand pounds of hay wagon roll over his chest. The fact that a hay wagon is loaded from back to front probably saved his life, the weight of the half-loaded wagon being mostly distributed across its rear wheels.

In any event, his sternum was crushed, he had a punctured lung, and more broken ribs than Dan can remember, but it would take more than that to keep him down. While everyone watched in amazement, Homer Ford stood up, dusted himself off, and walked over to his truck without asking anyone for help. He didn't even lay down in the bed of the truck. He got into the passenger seat sitting straight up and patiently waited for someone to drive him to the hospital.

Homer and Annie Ford, Gamaliel, Ky, 1920.

Old Blue and the Boys

If the reader has any mental image at all of a Tennessee walking horse, it is probably the iconic image of an impeccably groomed stallion in the show ring. This horse has ribbons braided into his mane to match the shiny brow band of a perfectly polished leather headstall. He has an impossibly long tail held slightly aloft with a leather strap attached to the back of the saddle to keep from dragging on the ground.

On his back is a perfectly postured rider wearing a riding jacket and a fedora perched on his head. He has polished leather riding boots on his feet complete with a set of blunt metal spurs. The horse in this image is usually captured mid-stride, exhibiting a perfect, four-beat running walk with three feet firmly planted on the ground and one foreleg held high in a curl as he reaches out for the next step. Horses like this had majestic names such as Generator's Major General, Pride of Midnight, or Dark Spirit's Rebel. Sometimes they evoked a diva effect with names like The Revelation, Motown Magic, or Sensational Shadow.

We did have some horses like this at Harlinsdale, and they were magnificent. Kept in the lacquered wood stalls of the Show Barn, they would be exercised several times a week, groomed impeccably, and turned out to graze in their own private grass paddock. Their names would be engraved onto matching wooden signs and affixed to their stall door. Their personal leather halters were kept separately from the rest and likewise adorned with a small brass plate engraved with their name and titles they had earned. Painted portraits of them hung in the office of the barn and their ribbons and trophies lined the book shelves.

But that's not the image that comes to mind when I think of a Tennessee walking horse.

The horse I'm thinking of has burrs and twigs stuck in his mane from riding through the woods and rolling in the dirt. His hair is slightly bleached by the sun from living his life out in pasture. His tail is shorter than his show horse cousin and doesn't have quite the same shine, but is still useful for its primary purpose of swatting flies. He wears an old leather bridle that may or may not match the saddle on his back, and a saddle pad chosen for comfort rather than style.

On his back is a perfectly relaxed rider, comfortably seated in a western saddle with one arm at his side and the other casually holding a loose rein. This rider wears blue jeans and work boots, a green and white Harlinsdale Farm hat perched high on his head. He wears no spurs and needs nothing but the imperceptible click of his tongue or a softly spoken, "Come on, boy" to get his horse moving along. These horses had names like Big John, Rusty, Liner, Apple Jack, Chip, Blaze, Blue, and Trigger.

They were all registered Tennessee walkers, tracing their lineage back through the same champion bloodlines to Midnight Sun as their show horse counterparts. They probably had fancy names on their registration paperwork, but they had earned new names—and new identities. These names meant something to the men who worked with them and bonded with them, and they were valuable in a way that a show horse never could be. They were big, stout, hardworking horses, and they were good riding horses—even if they may have preferred a hard pacing gait over a good running walk—but they were surefooted and trustworthy.

They were all geldings, meaning they had been castrated as two-year-olds. Geldings make great work horses, as they are no longer consumed with an obsession to procreate or exert their dominance over everything in sight. They could be worked in a field full of mares, or even turned out with them to live on pasture, and could work and live alongside their fellow geldings without any complications. That's not to say that they lost their personality; quite the opposite. Living their life as the working companions of the men of Harlinsdale, they seemed to consider themselves set apart from the herd. They made friends and had their favorites, both equine and human.

Apple Jack, for instance, would never be found more than a few inches from Liner. So much so that whoever was chosen to ride Apple Jack had almost no say in where the horse would go. It was just accepted than Apple Jack would follow Liner wherever he went. So close, in fact, that his nose was usually attached to Liner's tail as if he were a trailer. Apple Jack was a black horse with one glass eye. It was a functioning eye but it was crystal clear. He had a white blaze on his face and some other mismatched markings that might have counted against him as a show horse, but rounded out his personality perfectly as a Liner's goofy buddy.

Liner was a great big chestnut horse, bigger than any stallion at the farm. He was the preferred riding horse for the 6'4" Harlin Hayes. Mr. Hayes even had an extra-large western saddle made for him, and Dad remembers that almost no one else could ride him. His barrel was simply too large for any normal-sized human to get their legs around and find the stirrups. Matching Mr. Hayes in both size and personality, he was always the lead horse in any group.

Before Dad's time, there was Big John and Rusty. When Dad was a boy, Big John was already turned out at the Hillsboro farm in his retirement, but my grandfather would sometimes get Big John up and let the kids ride him. Rusty actually belonged to a Mr. Glover, who was allowed to keep him on the farm free of charge. Rusty earned his board by joining the work force with the other geldings whenever he was needed. These two were the working companions of the older generation of men like Homer Ford and Mr. MacArthur.

Blaze was my great-grandfather Wirt's horse. He was a light chestnut horse with a flaxen mane and tail and a white blaze down his face. Blaze lived a bit of a charmed life. He had the looks of a show horse but lacked any "get up and go," so my great-grandfather brought him home to be a pleasure horse. In an article highlighting scenes of the southern sporting culture, Blaze was featured on the cover of *Southern Living* magazine. As Wirt's favorite riding horse, he would travel with him to Florida in the winter to join the other snow birds soaking up the warmer weather. Later in life, he started to find himself in the line-up with the other working horses, something he did not appreciate. He would do his job, but it always seemed he might not be giving all he had, as if it were somehow beneath him.

Trigger was the gelding I remember riding the most when I was a teenager working on the farm. Trigger was a palomino-colored horse, taking his name from the similarly-colored mount of the singing cowboy Roy Rogers. Trigger was one of the most stubborn horses I have ever known. He would work hard, but he was always trying to figure out what had to be done just so he could be finished, and didn't seem to care whether you were there or not.

If he knew you were taking him out to round up mares, there was almost nothing you could do to slow him down. You might be able to steer him left or right, but mostly you were just along for the ride. It's not so much that he enjoyed it; he just wanted to get it over with. If we got all the way back to the barn before I realized we had missed a few mares, it took a considerable effort to get him to go back out into the field. He considered the barn to be home plate where he was safe from any further work requirements.

If you managed to get him all the way to the far corner of the back field and then pointed him even remotely back toward the barn, it was on. A number of times I had to steer him into the corner of a field while he ran flat out, and just hoping I could hang on when he came to a skidding stop just inches from the barbed wire. Other times we'd come down the hill in the back field, on the verge of running out of control, bearing down on a ninety-degree turn through an open gate flanked by barbed wire fence on three sides.

Trigger would hit that turn without slowing down, plant his front hooves and wheel around, dropping his hind end like a cutting horse and then explode again into a run. I could only try my best to get into rhythm and anticipate when he would plant his feet to make the corner, trying not to think about what it would feel like to go sideways through that wire. I wish I could say I was a better horseman and not merely a reckless one, but truthfully the only choice was to hang on and hope. Bailing out was an option, but experience had proven it to be generally worse than just staying on. And I must say, it was exhilarating and more fun than just about anything else I remember doing as a kid; I'm just glad that neither of us ever got hurt.

Blue was Dad's horse, and as he remembers fondly, they broke each other. He was a blue roan with two white stocking feet and a wide white blaze down his face that faded into a pink nose and muzzle. Dad got the opportunity to break him when he was a freshman in college and Blue was a two-year-old. He couldn't help but feel sorry for him after he was castrated, especially when he had to keep riding him while the surgical wound healed[1]. Dad would come down to the barn from Lipscomb University after school and on weekends and ride Blue everywhere—up and down the lane, out in the woods, and all through the fields.

There is an old wooden bridge that crosses a spring-fed creek about two-thirds of the way down the Lane toward the Upper and Lower Barns. This was a stout old bridge (that still stands today) that held aloft the narrow gauge railway of the old, inter-urban trolley. Taking a yearling across it by the halter was harrowing enough, the wooden planks making a deep hollow sound as their hooves stomped across it. I'm sure in their minds there was an alligator underneath waiting to jump up and eat them.

Blue remembered this bridge from his yearling training, and there seemed to be nothing Dad could do to get him across it. He could prod and kick at his sides, but nothing he could do would get Blue to budge an inch over those wooden planks. He couldn't even dismount and get Blue to follow him across on foot. He finally figured out that Blue would cross the bridge, but only backward. It took a few repetitions, but Blue eventually learned that bridge travel was actually safer going forward.

---

1 Open castration was the preferred method at the time, and while it may sound cruel, keeping the horse in regular work is the best way for the wound to drain and heal from the inside out without getting infected. Out of respect for the reader, I have omitted Dad's description of the sound this "wound" would make when he rode him…

While others would ride him if they needed to, Dad and Blue were bonded and everyone deemed him to be "Clay's horse."

Dad's generation used the geldings for work much more than me and my cousins ever did. During the early weeks of breaking yearlings, they would saddle up several geldings and use them as pony horses. They would head out in a group of five or six at a time with a yearling hitched to each saddle horn. The yearlings being at first skittish around people, they would be more be trusting of their gelding training partner and fall in line behind the other horses as they headed out across the fields. They would walk for miles, wearing down the yearlings until they could be hand walked by another farmhand. The riders would then hitch up a fresh colt and head out again.

These are Dad's fondest memories of working at Harlinsdale. With Liner and Mr. Hayes leading the way, Mr. Hayes would relax around the boys and let them enjoy the camaraderie and tell all the old stories, all the while teaching the younger men what he knew of horsemanship. He would question them about each colt, ask what they saw in them, and teach them what to look for in a quality horse.

Blue was also the horse Dad would get up when it came time to teach us kids to ride. He was steady and trustworthy and we all learned to ride on his back even before our legs were long enough to reach the stirrups. If we ever had a class field trip to the barn or had some visitors in town who wanted to ride, Blue was their assigned mount. He was still around in my early teenage years and would tear out across the field with reckless abandon right beside Trigger. By that time Blue must have been close to twenty-five years old, an elderly age for a horse.

Blue was in his prime during Dad's tenure at the farm in the late 1970s and '80s. In the fall and winter months, the Harlinsdale crew would turn to various maintenance tasks that had been alluding them all summer, mostly repairing fences and improving the barns. The farm out in Hillsboro was hilly and wooded in places and in these woods could be found groves of young locust trees. Black locust tree trunks are ideal for fence posts, growing upward of sixteen feet long and almost completely straight, with uniform thickness. The wood itself was also impervious to rot or insect infestation when buried in the soil.

If the felled trees were on the edge of the woods, then they could easily be gathered with a chain and dragged back to the barn with a tractor. They could then be trimmed of their branches and cut into eight-foot fence posts. One day, however, Dad and Rocky found a whole grove of nice, straight locust trees deep into the woods and down in the bottom of a ravine. Even though the ravine was too steep for a tractor, the trees were too good to pass up and so they cut them anyway, deciding they would figure out later how to get them out.

Rocky had grown up working farms with mules and horses and so naturally he had an idea. They loaded up Blue in a trailer and brought him out to Hillsboro the next day, fitting him into the harness that had been used to pull a ground sled with Homer's old mules. Blue had never worn a harness before, much less felt the pull of a heavy load attached to its traces.

They led him down into the ravine and bundled up a few of the cut trees and hitched them to the harness. Not quite sure what he was going to do, they urged Blue forward until he took out the slack from the traces. Without another word, Blue knew just what needed to be done and he hauled that first load straight to the top of the hill and out of the woods. He kept this up all day, load after load, at times losing his footing and driving up the hill on his knees until he could plant a solid hoof on the hill and continue on. In a way that no other horse had ever done, Blue had forever endeared himself to Dad with the strength of heart he displayed that day.

On other days, they would take a few geldings out to the Hillsboro farm to round up the mares that had been turned out or the herd of Hereford cattle that was kept there. The mares would spend the fall and winter out there while they waited the eleven months or so until their new foal was due to arrive. Rocky and Dad would have to round them all up for vet checks and routine health inspections, or perhaps to take one or two back to Harlinsdale for one reason or another.

To round them up they would have to go out all around the farm and drive them back to the barn. The mares generally followed the worn down tracks across the fields that marked the path of least resistance between various grazing spots and watering holes. These paths were never straight and meandered up and down the sides of hills, down through creek beds, and in and out of the woods. Perhaps out of a sense of obedience, or perhaps just to avoid being hassled, most of the mares would follow these tracks back to the barn without too much prodding. There were always a few however, that would be belligerent. They would want to get out front and turn the herd back, or break off into smaller groups and head off the path into a grove of trees to hide, or generally try and figure out what you were trying to do and find a way to not do it.

For the geldings, this was a lot of work but they were seasoned veterans. They knew if they didn't get behind the mares and keep them together, they would have to go back and do it again. They only had one shot to do it right the first time, and they would aggressively go after any strays, throwing their ears back and baring their teeth to drive home their displeasure with the troublemakers. If they saw an escape route, they would gallop ahead to cut the herd off and keep them on the trail.

For a gelding like Blue, Dad didn't have to do much but hang on and ride him. Blue knew when to speed the mares up or take the pressure off and slow them down. He knew how to get around them and cut them off, and could sense even before they did if there was some momentum about to take them in the wrong direction. Sometimes this cutoff might take Dad and Blue down a steep wooded hill, with fallen longs and hidden rocks underneath the overgrowth—conjuring up the climactic scene in *The Man From Snowy River*—but Dad trusted Blue and let him go where he needed to go.

And so, there he was. Dad and Blue were coming out of some woods onto a plateau as a herd of mares thundered out in front of them. Blue took off after them, maybe thirty or forty in the group, and they came to a place where Blue needed to beat them across an open space to keep them from getting away. As Dad remembers, Blue was particularly belligerent that day and he didn't like how close Blue was to being out of control. As Dad pulled back on the reins to slow him down and remind him that he was still in charge, the reins broke. Blue hauled out across the plateau and Dad was left with nothing but the dry, rotted ends of the old leather reins in his hands. Dad sunk his heels low into the stirrups and felt Blue surge forward, suddenly a race horse that had been opened up to full throttle.

Up ahead, Dad could see that Blue was intent on taking a line through the woods, a dense pocket of trees with large, low branches Dad could not possibly duck under. He imagined being cleaned off by one of these branches, or having one driven into his chest at thirty miles an hour, and he knew he had to do something fast. With only seconds to go before they crashed into the woods, Dad assessed the possibility that he might be about to die.

He reached down and grabbed a handful of Blue's mane with his right hand, and leaning as far forward as he dared, he grabbed the side of the headstall of Blue's bridle with his left. He pulled with all his might, bending Blue's head around nearly to where his nose touched Dad's knee. This finally broke Blue's intense concentration, no longer able to see where he was going. He slowed down as he was forced to turn in a circle, finally slowing to a walk, and Dad could dismount safely. Not that this meant his ride was over; they still had mares to round up. Dad tied the loose ends of the reins to the rings on the sides of Blue's bit, and the two of them headed out again, charging down the hill in full pursuit of the herd.

Descending the hill, the mares had chosen a line that crossed a shallow creek where the banks sloped gradually on either side. Blue still thought he could head them off by getting an angle on them and he chose a line that crossed the creek from higher ground where there was a drop of about five feet on both sides going down to the water. There was little to nothing Dad could do to influence Blue toward the easier crossing, and as the gap between the banks of the creek got closer, Dad could also see it was quite a long way across. Dad never had any interest in riding jumping horses like his sister Camille, and Dad wasn't sure old Blue had any experience with the sport either, but he was about to find out.

As they reached the near bank, Blue timed his stride perfectly and exploded across the gap. He barely made it, in fact only clearing it with his front end, and his back legs missing the far edge by mere inches. Blue had enough of a firm footing on the high edge to drive into the side of sheer bank with his back hooves, and kept moving forward up and out of the creek, and both horse and rider lived to ride another day.

It may sadden the reader to think these geldings did not enjoy any cushy retirement, no private stall, and a trough full of grain to live out their last few years in perfect comfort. There are no monuments to them or grave sites to visit. They died as they lived, as horses out in the open fields and rolling pastures of Harlinsdale Farm, and I know they wouldn't have had it any other way. They live on in fact, just as Harlinsdale lives on, in our hearts and in our stories and in all the ways they made us who we are. So here's to you Blue…and Trigger, Liner and Apple Jack, Chip, Blaze, Big John and Rusty, and all the geldings of Harlinsdale. You were good boys, you.

Clay holds Anna Beth on Blue, c. 1980.

Talbot and Trigger, c. 1987.

Clay leads Meredith on Blue, c. 1987.

Talbot and Blue, c. 1989.

Anna Beth helps secure Meredith on Sunny the pony; Faye on Trigger, c. 1987.

Harlin Hayes and his grandson John on Liner, c. 1963.

Wirt at age 92, on Blaze, 1978.

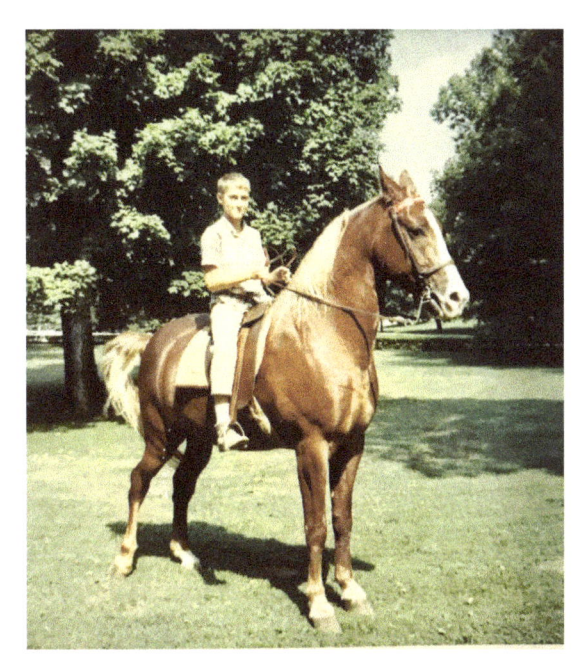

Clay on Blaze, c. 1968.

Clay leads Talbot on Sunny; Crystal and Reno supervise, c. 1985.

"If I couldn't do any better than that, I believe I'd quit."

-Rocky Jones

Automatic Post Hole Digger

I can't quite see through the fog of time to tell if I remember this correctly, but I think it was my cousin Bill at the wheel of the tractor when we clipped the fence post at the end of the Long Barn. It's possible I might have had something to do with it because I distinctly remember having to dig the hole to fix it. In any event, someone took the turn into the field too tight and the back right wheel of a completely full manure spreader caught that six-inch round post and snapped it like a toothpick.

Driving the tractor was a big deal. Pulling it up from one manure pile to the next as we threw out each barn was one thing, often more trouble than it was worth to fight anyone over the job. But once the manure spreader was full enough to be emptied, the competition grew fierce. The winner got to take the tractor and spreader rig out into one of the fields, engage the power take off, and send hundreds of pounds of horse manure and discarded shavings cascading out the back as you drove along, returning this organic material to the soil.

This job also had its risks. It is common farm law that whoever is at the controls of a piece of equipment when it stops working is the one who broke it, and nearly all the equipment at Harlinsdale was fraught with the risk of failing on any day. The driver also took upon himself the responsibility to maneuver this rig out to the field, sometimes backing it out of tight spots, in and around barns and fences that in most cases pre-dated the Second World War, and in some cases the First. These factors often weeded out the more risk-averse farmhands that didn't have "Harlin" in their name, something that entitled me and my cousins to a bit more job security.

Narrowing it down, it would have made sense for Bill to be at the controls that day. Being the elder cousin on the work detail, it was his prerogative to drive the tractor if he wanted to, only abdicating this role if he was in a mood to be generous or saw some other advantage to sitting it out. So, it's settled then. Bill was driving the tractor as we cleaned up the last manure pile at the northwest corner of the Long Barn. There was a more or less straight shot out into the field just north of the Long Barn that ran all the way down the Back Lane and then east to Franklin Road.

The gate opened from the southwest corner of the field, so to Bill's left as he drove through the opening. This field was used to turn out the mares and foals from the Long Barn, and someone would need to hold the gate open for the tractor and spreader and then close it after it was clear. The gate holder, presumably me, could not have seen the impending disaster as the doomed fence post would have been on the right side of the tractor and blocked from view.

The remaining farmhands on the work detail had either absolved themselves of any responsibility to watch the tractor clear the gate or were headed back to the Show Barn, toting all the scoops and pitchforks to put them away, as this would've been the last barn we had to throw out that day. I think we can all agree at this point that Bill was solely responsible for the calamity about to befall us.

Automatic Post Hole Digger

All I saw was the right side of the manure spreader jump about a foot into the air and I heard a crack as the wire fence warped with the weight of the now-broken fence post. It was an easy mistake, not taking a wide enough turn into the field—a task made more difficult by trying not to crash the front-end loader into the other side of the fence or clip the big oak tree in the corner. The lack of power steering also made this particular tractor tend to follow roots and ruts as it plodded along. With the nuisance fence post now out of its way, the spreader and tractor continued out into the field and the damage was clear to see—the post broken right at the ground level, laid out but held slightly aloft by the tension of the wire fence.

This was really not a big deal in the grand scheme of things; it probably happened dozens of times in the life of the farm. No one got hurt, no horses escaped, the tractor and spreader kept on keepin' on like nothing had happened. But to a group of young men entrusted to manage expensive and dangerous equipment without adult supervision, this seemed like it would have severe consequences.

A quick inspection of the damage eliminated any possibility of a cover up, and it was clear this would have to be fixed before any work continued. Horses, like toddlers, have a sixth sense when it comes to finding opportunities to engage in mischief. Already the herd of mares and foals had perked up from across the field, sensing the possibility of investigating a mess of broken wood and mangled wires they could stomp their feet into.

I don't remember who went and 'fessed up or what was said. The identity of the tractor driver didn't seem to matter to the judge or jury. Circumstantial evidence in this case was sufficient for a conviction and we were all found guilty. I assume reluctant forgiveness was offered after a few rounds of, "Use yer head for somethin' besides wearin' a hat!"

I do know that our punishment was to fix it—and so off we went to the Tractor Barn to fetch the required gear. The Tractor Barn was the old, inter-urban trolley station power plant that now served as a mechanical workshop, tool shed, and tractor storage facility among other things. Inside the shop was a veritable museum of farm implements going back a hundred years or more, some of them no doubt making the original pilgrimage down from Gamaliel.

There were old, wood-handled sickle blades and scythes as tall as a man; rusted chains holding handmade block and tackle; various shovels; rakes; scoops. There was an anvil attached to an old oak tree stump, and an old foot-powered stone wheel for sharpening these artifacts of nineteenth-century farming. Taking up most of the open bay were a couple of antique tractors that didn't work anymore except in the imagination of a young boy. One of them was undoubtedly the old McCormick W-9 that ran over Homer Ford in 1961.

There were also some more modern additions: lawn mowers, trimmers, tractor battery chargers, an electric bench-mounted grinder, and any conceivable size of wrench or socket scattered about with no discernible order. Somewhere laying around in there you could always find an old spare part for pretty much anything imaginable, from a trailer hitch pin to a chainsaw chain. It was here where we would have found a new fence post leaning against the wall, probably a six-inch diameter by eight-foot-long wood post treated with creosote.

We would have also found wire cutters, nails, hammers, and—most importantly—a post hole digger and a tamping bar. The former was basically two round-point shovels attached with a scissor joint in the middle and the shovel blades curving away from one another to form two halves of a cylinder. The latter was a metal bar about five feet long, with a flat blade on one end and a large, round mallet on the other, not unlike a giant, sixty-pound, flathead screwdriver.

The operator would take the post hole digger and smash it into the ground with the sharp end of the shovel blades then spread the two handles apart, causing the shovels to pivot toward one another, pinching the load of dirt between them. In this way, scoops of dirt about a quart at a time could be excavated from a hole that kept its cylindrical shape. Into this hole would eventually go the new post, filled in with rocks and dirt, and then incrementally tamped down with the round end of the aforementioned tamping bar.

Now this was before CrossFit™; little did we know we were ahead of the times when it would become a fitness phenomenon to pick up heavy things and pretend to do manual labor and call it a workout. This Workout of the Day (WOD) would have been called "post-hole shoulder makers" and "tamping bar power slams." This was a team exercise and would smoke any one person after a few minutes. I'm sure we traded out, which is how I must have found myself driving this post hole digger into the ground over and over, wondering how far down was far enough.

There must not have been much else to do just then because it also seemed we had acquired an audience, or at least more spectators than operators. Perhaps we had just forfeited the right to work unsupervised for the rest of the morning, but in any event, Rocky was there to make sure it was done properly.

Seeing that he was enjoying himself I said in a moment of exasperation,

"They should make something that does this, like an automatic post hole digger or something."

This is, of course, called an *auger*. I knew something like this existed even if I didn't know it's proper name—and anyway—I was just trying to make a point.

"They do," replied Rocky.

"Well then we should get one," I said.

"We got one," said Rocky.

"Well then we should use it!" I exclaimed.

Walked right into that one...

A smile crept over Rocky's face as he answered, "I am."

Harpeth River Submarine

My dad looked at the hard-packed ground in the Lower Barn. He had been sent down the Lane to "throw out those sheds," but now he was pretty sure there had been some mistake. But for a few dried up and nearly petrified horse droppings scattered around, it looked like what he imagined the floor of this old barn to be in its natural state. Just dirt.

Throw out what? He thought to himself.

It didn't look like any shed my dad had ever seen either, just a large, open wing of the barn that allowed twenty-five or thirty mares to run in at a time to get out of the weather and eat dry hay in the winter. They never really got cleaned out on a schedule, not until the summer help showed up, naively eager to get their hands into some farm work.

Thinking perhaps these barns had already been done and he was about to sneak a few hours of leisure time until someone figured it out, Dad sent his pitchfork into what looked like solid earth just to prove it to himself. Much to his dismay, he sunk all five tines of his fork into what was really a winter's worth of packed hay and manure, among other things. He stepped onto the top of the fork and rotated the handle down to see what it would turn up. The heat and intense smell of ammonia and decomposing organic matter nearly knocked him down. It was going to be a long day, and he was just getting started.

"Now look here, baby boy."

That was Mr. Parrish, Dave Parrish, who was in charge of this job. Dad wasn't sure yet where he fit into the pecking order, so he just called him Dave, but the other guys all called him Cousin Dave or just Cuz. It wasn't meant out of any disrespect; they meant it as a term of endearment. But Dad, just past his twelfth birthday and with only one summer at Harlinsdale under his belt, wasn't quite comfortable with that level of informality with a grownup.

Dave was using a scoop instead of a fork, a wide shovel with a large handle at the top to pick up much larger portions of manure for each of his efforts. Dave Parrish was of mixed heritage but most folks would have described him as a black man, and he was a big man. He was probably pushing his late sixties by this time, but he still had the strength of three men half his age. He scooped up a fifty-pound load and sent it sailing into the manure spreader, just to show Dad how it was done.

Dad really liked working with Dave; it was a reprieve from the bustling energy of the rest of the farm, where he kind of felt in the way. He was probably in Dave's way too, or it was safe to say he probably slowed him down a little, but Dave never made him feel that way. If Dad missed the manure spreader trying to toss a load from his pitch fork, Dave never gave him a hard time, just tried to show him a better way to do it.

If Dad put too much grain in the wheelbarrow at feeding time, making it too heavy for him to push, Dave never made him feel small or weak. He'd just make up some reason to switch jobs with Dad and give him something else he could handle.

Cousin Dave lived on Adams Street in Franklin, about two miles away, and he walked to work every day. Rain, sleet, or shine—every day. He called everybody *baby boy*; well, at least the teenage help that came down in the summer time. Day to day he worked for Mr. Irwin, Al Irwin, whom Dan Ford had taken to calling "Puss." Of course Dan was a little older than my dad, and could get away with stuff like that, having graduated from shed and stall cleaning duty. He had proven he could handle himself around a horse and was out with Mr. MacArthur catching mares for the breeding day.

Mr. Irwin and Dave didn't do much with the horses, like breaking yearlings or catching brood mares or anything like that. Mostly they were in charge of the day-to-day management of the farm work. In the summers, when the work force swelled with extra help, mostly high school boys, Mr. Irwin would send Dave out with his new recruits to knock out chores that had been alluding them all winter and spring. There were lots of boys older than Dad who showed up at the beginning of summer thinking they wanted to work at Harlinsdale. Chores like this had a way of testing that decision and most of them weren't around anymore.

Dan was one of the older boys who everyone knew was sticking around. He was also fun to work with and was always patient with Dad. Being a little closer in age, he could still sympathize with what it was like when he first started and had taken Dad under his wing. He had also warned Dad about Dave's stories.

"He'll tell you some stories if you get him started, I mean stories that can't be true, but he'll tell 'em like he really believes it hisself, so much so that you start to wonder if he's crazy. But he's not, he's very sane. But if you get him started he'll tell you anything."

"Like what?" Dad had asked.

"Like, when I first started here, that first summer, he had me goin' on that there were lions and tigers back up there on that bluff. Now I knew that warn't true, but the way he talked about it, I didn't go back there for nothin', 'cause he had me wondering—the way he talked about it—like he believed it. I heard him get your cousin Carter goin' on about how he kept some brand-new Cadillacs in a cave up there that only he knew about."

Dad had heard some of these stories too, even before he came to work at the farm. One day, Dave saw him headed out to the woods up on The Bluff with his .22 and Dave warned him to be on the alert. He had been up there a few days before and seen a group of rabbits marching around in military formation with rifles on their shoulder. Whenever Dave would see an airplane flying overhead, he would tell the boys about the time when he used to fly an airplane of his own with various famous people. He loved it when someone would follow up with a question meant to stump him or call him on his tall tale. Dave was always ready with a follow-up story that took his audience even further into his fantastic imagination.

Now, Dan could tell some stories too. Earlier that week Dan was telling everyone about a time, a few months earlier, how Mr. Hayes had Dan follow him to Gamaliel with a truck he'd bought—a big, two-ton truck that Mr. Hayes wanted for hauling horses. He was taking it up there to have a big, stout, heavy bed built onto it and he needed Dan to give him a ride back.

Of course, Mr. Hayes would never have done this on a work day, so he called Dan up after he got off from school one Friday and said to come out on Saturday afternoon and follow him up to Gamaliel. Well the catch was, according to Dan, they got there too late to drive back the same day and so they had to spend the night up at Mr. Hayes' momma's house[1], where apparently the guest quarters were limited.

"And I had to sleep with him…"

"…in the same?…"

"In the same bed. And he's what, six-foot-four, two sixty—maybe two seventy? In the same bed with me. And we didn't eat much for supper that night, and then we drove the whole way back the next day and that man didn't say but four words. We'd pass some place and I'd say, 'Man, I bet they got some good hamburgers in there.' Mr. Hayes just keep on drivin'."

They did get a nice bed put on that truck though. You could haul seven or eight full-grown mares, maybe ten yearlings. Dan was out in it now with Mr. Mac, probably taking a teasing stud out to one of the farms Harlinsdale had leased to accommodate their growing business. Dan told my dad he counted up one day, between all the farms they owned and rented and the partnerships they had with other trainers and breeders in the area, that they kept over five hundred mares around Franklin.

Well, apparently all five hundred mares had been through this shed last winter, because Dad was starting to seriously doubt his life decisions. He didn't have to do this; he was Mr. Harlin's grandson after all. He could just come down here and go riding with his cousins and then go on up to his grandmother's house for a cold drink and sit in the shade. But he wanted to be a horseman, like his grandfather and Mr. Hayes, and Mr. Ford and Mr. Mac, and all the men he looked up to. If this is what he had to do to prove himself around the farm, then he was determined to be one of the boys who stuck around.

Seeing as how they weren't going anywhere for a while, there didn't seem much harm in pulling on Dave's string.

---

[1] Edna Hayes, sister of Wirt Harlin and married to Vanus Hayes.

"Say Dave, you done any fishin' lately?" asked Dad.

"Now listen here, baby boy…" and off he went. The next thing my dad knew, he was on an adventure with Dave down by the river. Dave had caught hold of a giant catfish so big he could ride it. This one's name, apparently, was Jethro. Dad had heard variations of this one before. Dave was a prolific catfish wrangler and he had names for all the monsters he rode down the Harpeth.

"Oh, come on now…" said my dad, expecting Dave to crack a smile and let him in on the joke.

Instead, Dave took it to another level. Pretty soon the idea of Dave riding catfish down the Harpeth seemed mildly plausible compared to Dave's next tall tale—that he also kept a submarine in the river. Dad was just trying to work out how small a submarine would need to be to fit in the Harpeth when Dave mentioned, almost as an afterthought, that Dad's grandmother Luella was a regular part of his submarine crew.

"Now listen here, baby boy. I'm tellin' you I know every inch of that river. That river is deep, son, and that's how come I know where those big ole catfish hide. You gotta find 'em deep down in that river, that's how come I need that submarine," said Dave.

"Ok then, how come my grandmother went with you?" Dad asked as a wry smile spread across his face. He thought he'd finally gotten Dave cornered.

"Look here, baby boy, who do ya think owns that submarine? But she don't know how to drive it, see. That's how come I first came to work here for your granddaddy, 'cause everyone knew I could drive that submarine he done got for Mrs. Harlin."

Dad laughed to himself, but also turned over whether or not the river might be deep enough… but then again Dave wouldn't know how to drive a submarine, would he? Was he in the Navy or something? And even if he did, would his grandmother…? Dad imagined his grandmother holding the ladder on the sail of a submarine, climbing down into it while trying not to step on the hem of her dress. Maybe this was years ago when she was younger…

"Come on now, Dave, quit messin' with these boys and let 'em get back to work. Y'all gotta do that Upper Barn before dinner."

That was Mr. Irwin. He had apparently come to check on their progress. Mr. Irwin would boss Dave around quite a bit, and rightly so as he was his superior at the farm. But still, it did kind of put a damper on what was starting to be a good time. Maybe my dad was starting to see why Dan called him "Puss."

"You know, baby boy," Dave said, lowering his voice and casting a knowing glance at Mr. Irwin. "Back when Mr. Irwin and I was in the Army, he wasn't nothin' but a private. But I was the sergeant. I was bossin' *him* around…"

"Are you gonna do any work today?"

-Rocky Jones

(To be used when someone appeared to be completely done in from hard work)

It Ain't About Muscle

We grew and harvested our own hay at Harlinsdale. Between a couple of fields along the Harpeth River set aside for this purpose, and another two-hundred-acre farm my grandfather owned out in College Grove, we were able to put up enough hay to get through the year on our own supply. The bulk of this hay was put up in batches throughout the summer when we had the most hands to help.

I don't pretend to know anything about the science of planting, cutting, or raking hay, and I also can't sit here and tell you exactly what kind of hay we planted and harvested. That's not to say there wasn't a science behind it of purposeful planting of a nutritious blend of grass hay; I'm just saying that's not where I fit into the process so it never concerned me. I was nothing but a foot soldier, a grunt when it came to getting up hay.

It's not like it was on the calendar, not something you could see coming on a specific day, at least not from my vantage point. The day would start out like any other, everyone grabbing their favorite fork and scoop to start working through the barns throwing out stalls, but then you might notice something a little out of place.

Alfred, who was always prone to break off early from stall cleaning duty to hitch up the little John Deere to the manure spreader, would instead start the day by cranking up the big John Deere and checking its oil and topping its tank off with diesel. Oscar might be hobbling around with a grease gun, hitting all the fittings on the old square bailer and filling its magazine with rolls of baler twine. Granddaddy might be strangely early to the barn that day so he could hitch up the hay rake to the old International tractor and head out to the hayfield with it[1]. Sure enough, there would go Dad and Rocky in the flat bed Chevy, toting a train of hay wagons out to the field.

With a combination of excitement and dread it would sink in—we're "getting up hay" today. At fourteen years old, this was the first experience I had with a feeling that would follow me through my entire career in the Marines—that of knowing you were on the cusp of an extremely challenging and difficult time—perhaps an unspeakably miserable or dangerous time—and while you prayed that circumstances would make it go away, if it was going to happen you wouldn't miss it for the world.

I would feel it again, shouldering a heavy pack at the beginning of an all-night hump[2] through a frozen Virginia forest, knowing that the only way to keep the feeling in my toes was to keep moving, even as I fell asleep on my feet. Or again while briefing up a night mission in our squadron's ready room as I felt the ship buck and roll in a storm, knowing my evening would have to end with a landing on its dark and pitching deck.

---

[1] It seemed to me that my grandfather's favorite thing to do was cut and rake a hayfield. Some of my best memories of him are when he would kidnap me for the day to go out to our farm in College Grove and we would rake the cut hay into windrows.

[2] In the Marine Corps, a *Hump* is what regular people may call a ruck march—a formation march with full packs, weapons, and tactical gear covering a dozen or more miles.

Or in this case, feeling the sting of a hundred tiny blades cutting my forearms as I stacked another hay bale on the wagon, a bead of sweat rolling into one eye and resisting the urge to wipe it with my hay covered hand, knowing I would have to throw that same bale up into the hay loft and stack it again before the day was through.

The whole process was pretty efficient from my point of view, most of the prep work being done without interrupting the breeding schedule or the breaking of yearlings, which is why it was usually a surprise to me[3]. By the time the big John Deere was hitched up to the hay baler and headed out to the field, the hay would have been cut and spread to dry and then raked into windrows, sometimes doubled up depending on the density of the cut hay.

Alfred always drove the big tractor, without exception. Behind him came the red New Holland square hay baler, and behind that a wooden hay wagon with about a ten-foot-tall rack on the back serving as a foundation into which we would stack the hay bales like a Tetris puzzle.

Alfred would drive along, collecting the rows of cut hay into the hungry teeth of the baler, and out the back would come forty-to-sixty-pound bales, depending on how dry they were, in a roughly 2'x3'x1.5' rectangle bound together with hemp string.

The baler had a chute that extended just up and over the front end of the wagon. Two or three men on the wagon would take the hay bales off as they were pushed up the chute and stack them according to a design chosen for stabilizing a tower of bales eight or more high. Mind you, the entire train was in motion across an uneven field, so you had to keep your knees

---

[3] The timing of this was undoubtedly dictated by the weather, several dry days being needed to cure the hay out in the field so it wouldn't be wet and prone to molding in the hay loft.

flexed and your center of gravity low in order to not lose your footing while you worked.

The five summers I spent working the farm take up an outsized space in my memories as a young man. Likewise, getting up hay seems to have a larger place than it deserves, considering we only did it maybe three or four times in a given summer. Being chosen to go out to the hayfield was a mix of excitement and dread, like a day of battle. On one hand, I always wanted to get picked, taking my place on the wagon next to the real men. On the other hand, throwing out stalls with my buddies was okay too—so long as none of them got chosen in my place.

The life lessons taught in a July Tennessee hayfield were worth more to my dad than my actual usefulness to the team, so I know I took a few turns that first summer out in the hayfield. But more often than not I had to watch the battle from afar as me and the other rear-echelon types finished cleaning out stalls and waited for the wagons to come back to the barn to be unloaded. When I did get to go out to the hayfield, I probably had to do some punishment laps walking beside the wagon and picking up bales I dropped, or ones that failed to clear the ever-higher and higher layers of stacked hay and subsequently fell overboard. It would be a few years before I was called out to take my place in the first wave.

Now, it's not like you could get out there and load a couple of wagons and then ask to be traded out. If you went out to the hayfield, you were in it until you rode that last wagon back to the Barn. Someone bringing the empty wagons out to trade for the full ones might offer to take your place, but the proper response was always, "Naw, I'm alright." This mindset was Rocky's fault. He would never quit, and would never be traded out. Whether it was hay, or working colts, or anything, his work ethic was the rising tide that floated all boats. He wouldn't say anything if you wanted to quit or take a break; he'd just keep on working. That was his leadership style and if you had any pride in your value as a worker, you wouldn't quit either. The last thing you wanted to hear was Rocky say, "Talbot, you go on back with this wagon."

If you were to wander into the hallway of the barn around quitting time on a day like this, you'd see two completely different groups of men. The men who practiced proper form and technique would be fairly worn out, a collar of sweat on their shirt, but otherwise relatively clean and free of cuts and scrapes. Rocky and Dad would look just like they did when they showed up that morning. Then you would see another group covered in bits of hay and dirt, completely smoked and streaked with brown filth from wiping hay dust from their sweat-covered faces, and with forearms that looked like they had been lashed with a cat-o-nine-tails. The latter group usually comprised the younger, fitter, and more athletic-looking fellows. That's because throwing hay bales wasn't about muscle.

Now don't get me wrong, at fourteen years old and a hundred and twenty-five pounds, I lacked both technique and muscle. Determined to keep up the pace and not get sent back to the barn, my only real chance was to try to do a clean and press over my head as the sharp stalks stabbed my arms and a shower of loose hay fell onto my face. This result was self-correcting and it required no formal instruction from the men who practiced the proper technique. Watching them work, it was evident that with a stiff arm swing and using very little muscle, save only a strong grip on the strings, and by rotating the torso to generate speed—all that was left was a properly-timed hand release and the hay bale would go sailing seven rows up and land softly in its place.

A veteran could pick his spot from the ground and land a hay bale right where it needed to be stacked, leaving the man on the top of the pile nothing to do but tamp it down into place. Not being tall enough at fourteen for this method, and not having the arm strength to throw it outright, that first summer I would stubbornly shrug it onto my thighs and then rotate it onto my forearms as I straightened my back and tried to muscle it over my head. This meant my pants would be brown from dust and sweat, my arms would be cut up, and my shirt would have about half a bale of hay inside it, making the skin on my chest and back crawl.

A Tennessee hayfield in the summer has its own weather— by that I mean about fifteen degrees hotter and fifty percent more humid than the ambient air just outside it. You could literally feel the heat radiating from underneath the wagon. Whatever breeze was in the air that day was guaranteed to come from directly behind the wagon at exactly its current speed and direction, leaving everyone in a perpetual cloud of hay dust with no relief from the heat.

Most everyone wore cloth gloves to protect their hands from the hemp strings and to avoid the unforgettable experience of having a sharp hay stalk shoved under their fingernails. After about fifteen minutes, these gloves would be useless for wiping any sweat from your face as they would be barbed with the tiny bits of sharp hay that stuck to anything soft. Since I was at first terrible at throwing hay bales, my arms and anything else I could think of to wipe away sweat would likewise be covered in hay. Therefore, within the first hour I would be down to one useful eye at any given time as I continuously blinked a sweat bead out of the other.

One by one we stacked bales, using an alternating method of long ends and short ends so that just part of the last bale in a row hung over the side, and the next layer would employ the opposite pattern of long and short ends so its weight would hold down the layer below it without any seams that could cause it all to tip over and fall. A well-stacked hay wagon could handle a bumpy and swaying ride back to the barn without losing a single bale and without any ropes holding down it's twelve-foot-high load. When the last wagon was loaded, the last windrow of loose hay consumed by the bailer, the triumphant warriors could ride atop the wagon stacked with hay back to the barn.

Forearms burning, eyes narrowed against the sweat and the sun, finally feeling that finicky breeze on your face that had been following you around all day, you swayed back and forth with the motion of the wagon as it plodded along across the now-bare hayfield. You might pretend for just a few minutes that your work was done, that you had finally gripped the last pair of hemp strings in your numb fingers that day. Then you'd round the corner of the barn and see a terrible sight—several stacked wagons yet to be unloaded. I'll never figure out how the math worked out, but the six guys unloading hay wagons into the loft while three guys loaded them up in the field always ended up about two wagons behind at the end of the day.

So you shake out your burning forearms, pull a few of the sharper barbs from your gloves, grab a handful of strings, and get back to work throwing hay bales. The camaraderie of the end of the day was always welcome, even if there was still work to do. Everyone back together again brought good-natured ribbing and the opportunity for feats of strength as the throwing platform got lower and lower as the wagon was unloaded.

I remember distinctly when I finally developed the right combination of strength and form to toss a hay bale from the bare wood floor of the wagon all the way up to the loft with one swing. It wasn't that first summer, I can assure you of that.

Back then I probably should have tapped out around the third or fourth layer down and taken my place up in the loft with the boys. But not before trying and failing first, of course.

Square up to the bale, feet shoulder-width apart, face away from your target, placing it just over your left shoulder. Try and get a good back swing to the right, maybe a little dip in the knees to generate momentum on the forward swing to the left, get the bale moving as fast as you can and then somewhere around the apex of that swing—let it fly. About halfway up on your swing you generally knew if it was going to make it all twelve feet up or not.

You also had to account for the inevitable fake flatulence or comical grunting coming from the spectators who were trying to get you to lose your focus and whiff. At fourteen, I'm sure that bale hit about four feet from the bottom of the hay loft and crashed to the ground. The floor of the hay wagon was about hip high, so maybe three feet off the ground. Now that a hay bale had fallen all the way down, and thus three feet further from the loft, the only thing to do would be to get down, set it back up on the wagon, and try again. And that's when I saw something I will never forget.

Hobbling around the wagon and raking up bits of hay from the Show Barn floor, was Oscar. Now Oscar, like I've said, was probably eighty years old. He would throw out stalls at a pace of about one of his to three of anyone else's. He rarely used a manure scoop to pick up piles because he couldn't bend over. He might take the better part of five minutes climbing up onto the tractor while we were scooping up manure piles, and usually we had picked up all the piles around the spreader by the time he got back down, so he'd just start the process all over again. If you asked him to go get a 'weed eater' he'd first go get a tractor so he could bring it to you perched in the bucket of the front-end loader rather than carry it.

Stories of Oscar pre-dated me at Harlinsdale by a couple of decades, so I'll leave it to other storytellers to attest to his work ethic in general; all I'm telling you is that he was as old and slow as you might expect for a man of his advanced age. But on this day he left me and my buddies and cousins staring at him in awe.

Oscar hobbled over to this fallen hay bale, contorted his body into enough of a bend to reach the strings, and picked it up with his bare hands. With a perfect back swing, he rotated his arthritic body around and launched this thing from ground level all the way up to the loft, clearing the edge by a foot or more and landing it squarely at the feet of an astonished teenager standing twelve feet above him.

"I been tellin' y'all boys," Rocky said. "It ain't about muscle."

"You see a boy around here, you step on him."

-Dan Ford

(In response to a pompous visitor who barked an order that began with, "Hey boy...")

$196

I'm not complaining; at the time I would probably have done it for free. I just wanted to be there, to be a part of the ongoing story. But $196 was the sum total of my first paycheck for a week's work at Harlinsdale. That's Monday through Friday, 7:30 a.m. to 5:30 p.m., and Saturday 7:30 a.m. until noon. This of course, doesn't count the thirty minutes or so before and after work when we commiserated about the day ahead or behind us. If anyone ever brought up the irregularity that Granddaddy only based our paycheck on eight hours a day while we worked closer to ten, he would highlight the fact that we only worked half a day on Saturday. So maybe we came out an hour ahead after you account for a lunch break, but I'm not sure I ever saw a pay statement to verify that assertion. It was more like a salary job based loosely on an hourly rate.

Payday was always on Saturday. Granddaddy would walk the farm chatting with each of us with a front pocket full of checks. It was explicitly clear that you were never to speak to another farmhand at Harlinsdale about what you got paid—that was strictly between you and him. I always thought it was a nice touch to personally speak with each employee and give him his paycheck rather than just leaving it in an envelope somewhere for us to pick up.

The minimum wage in Tennessee in 1995 was $4.25, and of course Granddaddy took out taxes. I don't ever remember any negotiation about pay when I asked him if I could work at the farm. Come to think of it, I don't remember that day at all, but I'm certain my dad made me formally ask for the job just as he had done. As the years went on I know my pay went up, and if my memory is correct I think I maxed out at around $375 a week. I'm sure he had better financial arrangements with the grown men based on their position at the farm, but he drove a hard bargain. Nothing was free at Harlinsdale except hard work.

Being part of the payroll went a long way toward making my contributions that first year seem official, even though I probably took away more than I gave. This wasn't like your granddad slipping you some cash to come hang out with him for the day under the pretense that you were there to work. This was on the books, a real check from Harlinsdale Farm's ledger with a W2 and everything. After the checks were handed out, we all broke off and made a run to the bank. It goes without saying that this was before the Internet and direct deposit, so if the guys wanted their money for the next week they needed to cash it or deposit it by noon. This also involved a stop at the gas station across from the farm for a celebratory Gatorade.

$196 for a week of blistered hands, stinking clothes, dust-covered skin, aching muscles, and sore feet. What I also earned was an appreciation for hard work, the driving desire to outwork everyone else, and for people to want me to be part of the team when a hard time came along. I learned to drive tractors, throw hay bales, work a front-end loader, and drive a stick-shift truck.

Most valuable to me and something that will be with me the rest of my life, I learned horsemanship. I learned how to earn a horse's respect, to read its eyes and body language, to control an animal that by all rights of its size and power should be out of my control. I learned what it felt like to struggle with a headstrong yearling for hours, not sure if it would ever give in, and then finally, with a lowered head and perked ears tuned to my voice and nothing else, a subtle motion with its nose toward my outstretched hand to say they were ready to try and trust me.

I learned that wisdom usually comes from men who speak the least, and is often found by keeping your own mouth shut. I learned that a horse doesn't care how big and strong *you* think you are, it only matters how big and strong *he* thinks you are. I learned humor and laughter can be found in the most miserable of times, and that part of being a good horseman was keeping your composure no matter how scared or tired or frustrated you might be. I learned that a true leader doesn't need to raise his voice, and a truly valuable man doesn't need to be told what to do.

I learned that no matter what, no matter which course my life took, I would forever be grounded at Harlinsdale Farm. I was determined to be a horseman, and I was forever changed. I would spend the rest of my life, no matter where I found myself, wishing I could draw in a lungful of air and be transported back to that place where the musty smell of hay and horses and that old barn tranquilized me.

"Use your head for something besides wearing a hat!"

-Harlin Hayes

The Veteran

In early June of 1970, Dad had just turned seventeen and completed his sophomore year at Battle Ground Academy. He drove himself to the barn now, of course. His days of catching the bus to Franklin were thankfully over. He parked his 1966 Ford Mustang under the shade of the trees that lined the turnout pasture just east of the Show Barn. He walked slowly toward the marble entryway, trying to savor the cool morning air before it faded into a hot Tennessee summer day. This was his seventh summer at Harlinsdale and he felt very much like a veteran now, no longer apprehensive around these men or the horses. He felt like he belonged here, finally, and he was really looking forward to this summer.

Those first few years he rarely got to handle the horses, usually being consigned to stall-cleaning duty or maintenance tasks. Sometimes they would use him as a runner to go out and be a human shepherd dog, rounding up fields full of mares. The thought had occurred to him that they were probably messing with him, because he was so eager and would do just about anything with alacrity. He would run his legs off, tearing out across the field all the way to the back corner to get around the farthest mare out in the pasture. The older hands would hardly break into a trot, just stroll out and around the field in a large circle, slowly closing the net on the herd to corral them toward the open gate as Dad pushed them out of the field.

He also realized that those first few summers they had shielded him from getting hurt, from letting him bite off more than he could chew. It must have been his second or third summer when they started to let him catch mares and bring them to the breeding shed. It was not hard to figure that he was given very specific ones to catch, obviously the most docile and gentle of the bunch.

If the orders came out of the breeding room to catch two or three at a time, one of the older guys would make sure he got one he could handle or swap with him if it looked like he had his hands full. More than a few times he had to surrender a mare to a more experienced horseman halfway back to the barn. What seemed unfair at the time was really just the older guys making sure he didn't have an experience that would leave him afraid and timid. Horses can sense fear in your touch and body language and confidence was paramount, or so he had learned.

Mr. Hayes was more like a drill sergeant to the "boys" than a farm boss. That is to say, he took it upon himself to train and protect them as they learned. Sometimes it seemed like he was just being tough on them, but the more Dad learned, the more he realized just how dangerous this job could be and how much of that responsibility Mr. Hayes bore on his shoulders. The young guys always felt invincible and naturally wanted to prove themselves, which meant they invariably put themselves in precarious situations. Mr. Hayes was careful to let them make mistakes so they could learn, but not such that they injured themselves unnecessarily, or worse, one of the horses. Hurt is one thing; injured is another. Mr. Hayes would always stand aside if you wanted to do something the hard way, and sometimes a good hoof to the shin was worth more than any correction he could give with words.

Dad sometimes felt especially singled out by Mr. Hayes; but, after all, they were family. With the hindsight and wisdom of age, he would grow to understand that this extra attention came from a place of genuine care for his growth as not only a farmhand, but a man. Dad would never forget the first time he got pawed in the face by a yearling. Getting "pawed" is an especially hilarious euphemism, as if a kitten were playfully patting your head with its soft furry feet. In this case, it was a term used to describe a horse that rared up and struck out with its front hooves, like giving Mike Tyson (in his prime) a pair of cast iron pots to hit you with.

On this particular day, Dad approached an especially wild yearling from straight ahead instead of the proper way he was taught. Mr. Hayes had shown him how to position himself to the left side of the horse and slip his hand under her chin and over the nose on the far side of her face. Using this method, his body would stay out of the engagement zone for either a fore or hind end attack. He could use his hand as a sort of human halter to hold the horse's head firmly tucked into its chest while using his free hand to slip the halter up and over her head. His right shoulder would always stay firmly in contact with the colt's left, so any movement by the horse to trample him would naturally push him out of the way before he got stepped on.

Deciding that maybe this was all just a little too much caution for an experienced horseman like himself, Dad figured he had enough mojo to just walk right up to this filly and slip the halter over her ears, standing directly in front of her. But as the hand holding the halter moved up her nose toward her eyes, she reared up on her hind legs and struck him square in the face with both front hooves. His eyes went blind with a flash of pain and shock as he staggered backward. Immediately, his face began to swell at the bridge of his nose and one eye.

He was scared and addled, his mind racing through all the possible trauma that horse might have just done to his head. When he finally regained his sight he saw the last thing he wanted to see: Harlin Hayes standing in the stall door. He anticipated at the very least hearing a sympathetic, "Are you alright?" Instead he got chewed out, Mr. Hayes laying out an irrefutable case for why this was Dad's fault and ending the lecture with, "Start using your head for something besides wearing a hat!" Instead of sympathy or first aid, Mr. Hayes had Dad pick up the halter and lead line, gathered everyone around, and made Dad do it again. Correctly this time.

Later in the day, when no one else was around, Mr. Hayes looked at Dad's swollen face and chuckled, "She really popped you a good one." It's not like Dad could really be mad at him. After all, Mr. Hayes had painstakingly shown him how to catch a horse and *not* get pawed in the face.

There were very few injuries around Harlinsdale that weren't ultimately the injured man's own fault. The part that Dad couldn't stop turning over in his head was how Mr. Hayes could have walked into that same stall, just the same way he had, and caught that colt with nothing but a firm voice and a "Whoa, now." Mr. Hayes was a big and imposing man—that was not in doubt—but moreover, he had a mystical power over horses. Dad had learned the hard way that this power came with experience, not audacity.

With the memories of past summers flooding back to him as he crossed the lane into the Show Barn, Dad heard a welcomed voice. The Harlinsdale crew was a stoic bunch; there wasn't usually much laughter coming from the hallway at this time of the morning. The guys generally sat around staring at the wall over the head of the man sitting across from them, sometimes uttering three- and four-word sentences, but only about once every two minutes or so. Today, however, Dan Ford was back.

Dan had been drafted into the Army in 1967. He would come back and visit when he was on leave, usually working for a few days to earn some money, but really just to feel the camaraderie of Harlinsdale again and feel at home. There was a time when people thought Dan might make a career out of working at the farm, maybe even take over for Mr. Hayes one day. Now twenty-one and his service in the Army complete, he had gone to work for the Nashville Electric Service and would eventually settle into the truck driving profession like his father. Of course, he was always welcome back at Harlinsdale and would usually find a few days or weeks in the busy summer months to help out with the yearlings and catch up with his Harlinsdale family.

Dad took his seat to a few nods and smiles from the other guys, their way of saying "Hey! Clay's here! Good to see you again! We're really happy to have you back around the farm this summer!" They didn't actually say any of this, but Dad knew what they meant. Just then Dan was in the middle of a story and no one wanted to interrupt him anyway.

"Well, Daddy come back from running that load of horses up there to Canada, to the French part of it, and he kept goin' on sayin', 'Did you know they speak a funny language up there?' and I'd have to tell him, 'Daddy, when you was up there, you were the one speaking a funny language!' But you know how Daddy is, once he gets something in his head you can't get it out. Y'all remember that gal he used to call Meridian, but that wasn't her name, what was it…"

"Meredith?"

"Yeah, that's it, Meredith, but he'd just keep on callin' her Meridian to her face, never once wondering why no one else called her that. Shoot, he had me calling her that too, and I didn't know it for years. Well anyway, he kept telling us when he was up there in Canada, 'Boy you know they drink some kinda strange coffee up there at night. I'd have one cup of it and just plum go to sleep,' and I had to tell him, 'Daddy, you know they was putting Cognac in your coffee!'"[1]

Knee slaps and laughter echoed through the barn as Dan talked, a stark contrast to their usually silent meditations. It wasn't that these men didn't like a good story or a conversation; it was just hard to find one of them who was willing to start it. That was Dan's forte. Dad had missed the first part of the story, but it didn't really matter; he laughed along anyway, just joyful to be back among this group of men. There was Herman MacArthur, Al Irwin, Howard Gamble, Haynes Sparkman, Oscar Pruit, Randy Baker, and of course, Mr. Hayes.

There was a new face in the group, which in and of itself was not remarkable. There were always a few who Dad didn't know very well, one of the various other high school boys who showed up for the first few weeks of summer before they realized they had made a big mistake. This newcomer was a tall, wiry, tough-looking kid. He had a quiet, confident way about him and it wasn't hard to figure he was no stranger to hard work. Dad had met him before, during a few Saturday visits to the farm over the previous spring. They had eyed each other warily, each not sure what to make of this other new fellow. His name, Dad had learned, was Rocky Jones.

---

[1] Clark Ford did not drink alcohol, intentionally at least.

Emery "Rocky" Jones, 1954—2019.

"Now let me tell you something about rocky: He was a man of his word. If he told you a mouse could pull a house... Hook him up."

-Dan Ford

Heir Apparent

There were two distinct epochs in the life of Harlinsdale Farm. In the beginning, there was Harlin Hayes. His almost mythical presence defined the era stretching from the birth of the farm until his death in 1980. Impossible for anyone to know at the time, but the arrival of Rocky Jones in the winter of 1969–1970 would mark the beginning of a new era that would last until the death of Harlinsdale in 2004[1]. I never knew the farm without Rocky; the two are forever intertwined in my memory. Older generations would say the same about Mr. Hayes. The two men were so remarkably similar—sparing in words, demanding in work, impeccable in leadership, natural-born horsemen—that I feel like I knew them both.

    The truth is, what I know about Rocky's life before and outside of Harlinsdale I only know from men who spent many more hours with him than I would ever be privileged to have. He was always inquisitive and interested in what I had been up to at school, what my plans were after, what I thought was funny or interesting. When the mood did strike him for conversation, it always got my attention and I tried to keep it going for as

---

[1] In truth, the business operation continued until around 2012 after moving it out to our farm in College Grove. The soul of it all, for me and Dad anyway, died at Harlinsdale in 2004.

long as I could. But like a young, enlisted man suddenly being given the attention of the old veteran sergeant major, it never occurred to me to ask him about himself.

Young people often struggle with a frame of reference that goes back further than their own consciousness and it seems we only ever talked about present and future. What I wouldn't give for a long ride out to College Grove in that old flatbed Chevy with Rocky today, to see if maybe as a grown man he might trust me with some of the more personal details about his early life. Such as it is, we will have to make do with what my father and Dan remember about him, and such details as his family has shared with us over the years.

Rocky grew up the hard way, working on sharecropper farms out in the hills west of Columbia, Tennessee. His boyhood was spent working those fields with mules and horses, growing a few acres of tobacco to squeeze whatever income they could out of the land. His father was in poor health and most of the responsibility to provide for his two brothers and three sisters fell to Rocky by age fifteen.

Mr. Irwin had some connection with the family and saw something in Rocky that deserved to be nurtured and rewarded. He recommended to Mr. Hayes that they bring him on and allow his family to move into one of the homes on the farm. There were four houses on the property and Rocky and his family moved into the one next to Mr. Irwin on the south side of the lane leading to the Show Barn.

Rocky was a born horseman, something Mr. Hayes and my great-grandfather recognized immediately. It was also impossible to ignore his determination to work harder than anyone expected him to. He was still in high school when they first moved to Harlinsdale, but Rocky would feed all the barns and fields before and after school every day. He would work the half day on Saturday with the rest of the guys, and then make himself available after hours the rest of the weekend for anything else that needed to be done.

There were always horses that needed routine doses of medicine at all hours of the night, boarders showing up on weekend afternoons to drop off or pick up horses, and in the foaling season there were mares who often needed someone to watch over them at night. Rocky took on any and all of these chores without complaint. When school let out for the summer he came to work full time like everyone else.

Rocky wasn't one to share much information, to say he was careful with his words was an understatement. He would sometimes spend an entire day without ever really talking to anyone, just thinking on things and working incessantly. He would communicate by doing, not ever wondering if anyone would follow his lead. After lunch he wouldn't announce that it was time to get back to work or even what we were about to do. He'd just appear out of nowhere holding a lunge line, stare at everyone for a second, and then stride off toward the truck and get in the cab. Translation: We're going down the lane to start working colts; now get your lunge line and get in the truck. The truth is, Rocky didn't have to say anything for you to know what he was about.

There were two things he valued—his work and his word. If he told you something, that's how it was. He would never gossip about anyone or suffer those who did. He would tell you the truth, and if he didn't think you'd like it he just wouldn't tell you anything. If he didn't know you, he probably wouldn't talk to you at all. I realize this makes him sound rude or arrogant, but that couldn't be further from the truth. Rocky lived on another plane, and there was a reason for everything he did. He hadn't grown up with the luxury of small talk or using his time in a meaningless way. He naturally took to men who could understand where he came from, and he probably shared a lot more about himself with Dan than he ever would with Dad. My father came from a different world than Rocky did, and there was always a barrier between them that only time could break down.

That's not to say Rocky was always uptight; the truth is he could be hilarious when he wanted to be. He always seemed to get you to stop thinking about the humidity and the heat and the stinging rope burns in your hands with a funny one liner or his high-pitched laugh, reminding you not to take yourself so seriously. His wit was always perfectly delivered, whether to make light of a hard time or painful mistake and encourage you to shake it off, or to get you out of your own head before you got yourself in more trouble.

In stark contrast to the Rocky I knew—perpetually capped in a Harlinsdale Farm hat with little to no hair and driving a white Ford F150—when Dad first met him he had a full head of long hair and drove a white Ford Falcon. As you might imagine for two teenage boys, there was a thinly veiled rivalry that existed between them. They sort of eyed each other cautiously for a while, Rocky probably thinking Dad was a pampered city boy who was going to try and slack off or throw his weight around because his granddaddy owned the farm. Dad, knowing what this country boy probably thought of him, was determined to prove that while he might have been born with a silver spoon, he'd traded it in for a pitchfork long ago.

This rivalry slowly turned into respect and then competition. Rocky didn't broadcast that he was trying to outdo you, letting you know beforehand that the competition had commenced, or that there even was one. He just did it. Whether it was working colts, getting up fields of hay, saddle breaking two-year-olds after the sale, or showing yearlings at horse shows, Rocky was trying to beat you whether you knew it or not. I don't mean he was trying to beat you to keep you down, but he would make you work harder and longer to keep up with him. If you wanted to take a break between colts and sit in the shade and get a drink of cold water, you'd look out into the field and there was Rocky, already working his next colt. If you waited any longer you'd see him circling the air over his head with his finger pointed at the sky, giving the signal for "Get you another one and get on out here."

In the late summer, the guys would take the best of their crop of yearlings to the local horse shows around middle Tennessee. Leading their colts into the show ring, Rocky would tell Dad, "I'm going to be right on your ass the whole class; don't take it personal." Of course Dad "took it personal" and would be so focused on out-showing Rocky that he forgot about all the other competitors. More often than not, they would steal the show trying to beat each other, not leaving much room for the other showmen in the ring so that at least one of them would be leaving with a blue ribbon. If it happened to be Dad, Rocky was always gracious in defeat, but he'd never hold on to a second place ribbon. If it wasn't blue, Rocky didn't want it.

My father would spend every summer at the farm working with Rocky until he graduated from Lipscomb University in 1976. After the yearling sale ended that summer, Dad's welcome at the farm ran out and he received the same treatment his father was given in 1946. That is to say, the family business was not a hand-me-down and he needed to go out into the wilderness and make his own way for a while. His true calling in life was that of a Christian minister and pastor, but he wouldn't find a way to make that his livelihood until well into his fifties.

My grandfather had designs on bringing him up through the ranks at his industrial laundry business, ostensibly to take over for him one day and keep the business running during his retirement, but Dad wasn't interested. He knew enough about himself at twenty-three years old to know his heart just wouldn't be in it. His heart was at Harlinsdale. So Dad worked for a few years in real estate but he always returned to the farm to work the annual yearling auction at the end of every summer. He refused to be sidelined from life at Harlinsdale and made it a point to be responsible for weekend foal watch and any after-hours appointments with boarders and clients who wanted to pick up or drop off horses after work on Saturday or Sunday.

By 1979, my grandfather and his brother Tom were managing the business decisions of Harlinsdale from afar as my great-grandfather was now well into his nineties. Mr. Hayes was running the day-to-day operations until 1980, when at the age of sixty-nine he passed away tragically from cancer. Dad had just moved his small but soon-to-be growing family into a new home in Franklin, just about two miles from Harlinsdale. My grandfather was still not ready to retire from running his business in Nashville and his brother Tom had moved out to another farm on the south side of Franklin. Harlinsdale was now in need of a Harlin, and Dad knew just where to find one.

What it didn't need, as he would soon come to realize, was a new leader. Dad was finally where he had always wanted to be, and he would make an indelible mark on the walking horse industry, on Harlinsdale Farm, and on everyone who worked with him through the years. But my father is a humble man, sometimes to a fault, and he could see just as well as anyone else that the best person to manage Harlinsdale going forward was Rocky Jones. Rocky was supremely talented and uniquely qualified to fill the gaping hole left by the loss of Mr. Hayes.

Many men idolized and aspired to be Mr. Hayes, my father and grandfather not least among them, but there was really only one man who could fill his shoes.

That's not to say that Harlinsdale wasn't in need of Dad's own unique talents. Dad is a natural at forming relationships and endearing himself to people, leaving aside his talent and experience as a horseman and salesman. My grandfather was a firm believer in the "Peter Principle"—that to promote someone past their point of maximum contribution and natural talent in an organization was a mistake, and would frustrate both the individual and the business. While he had an ulterior motive to drive his youngest son into the corner office at his industrial laundry business, and one day he would succeed, even he could not argue that it would take both Dad and Rocky to pull Harlinsdale forward into the next chapter. From 1980 onward, they would breathe new life into the farm, attracting new clients and forging new relationships with trainers and owners around the industry.

It was during this era that I also entered the picture, a young boy tucked in behind my dad down at the Barn on Saturday mornings, or riding out with him on Sundays after church. My earliest memories are of rolling around in a straw pile with our Australian cattle dog Crystal's new litter of puppies, riding our pony "Sunshine" around in the hallway of the barn, and strutting around in my little cowboy boots and jeans with an oversized Harlinsdale Farm hat perched on my little head, determined to be just like my dad.

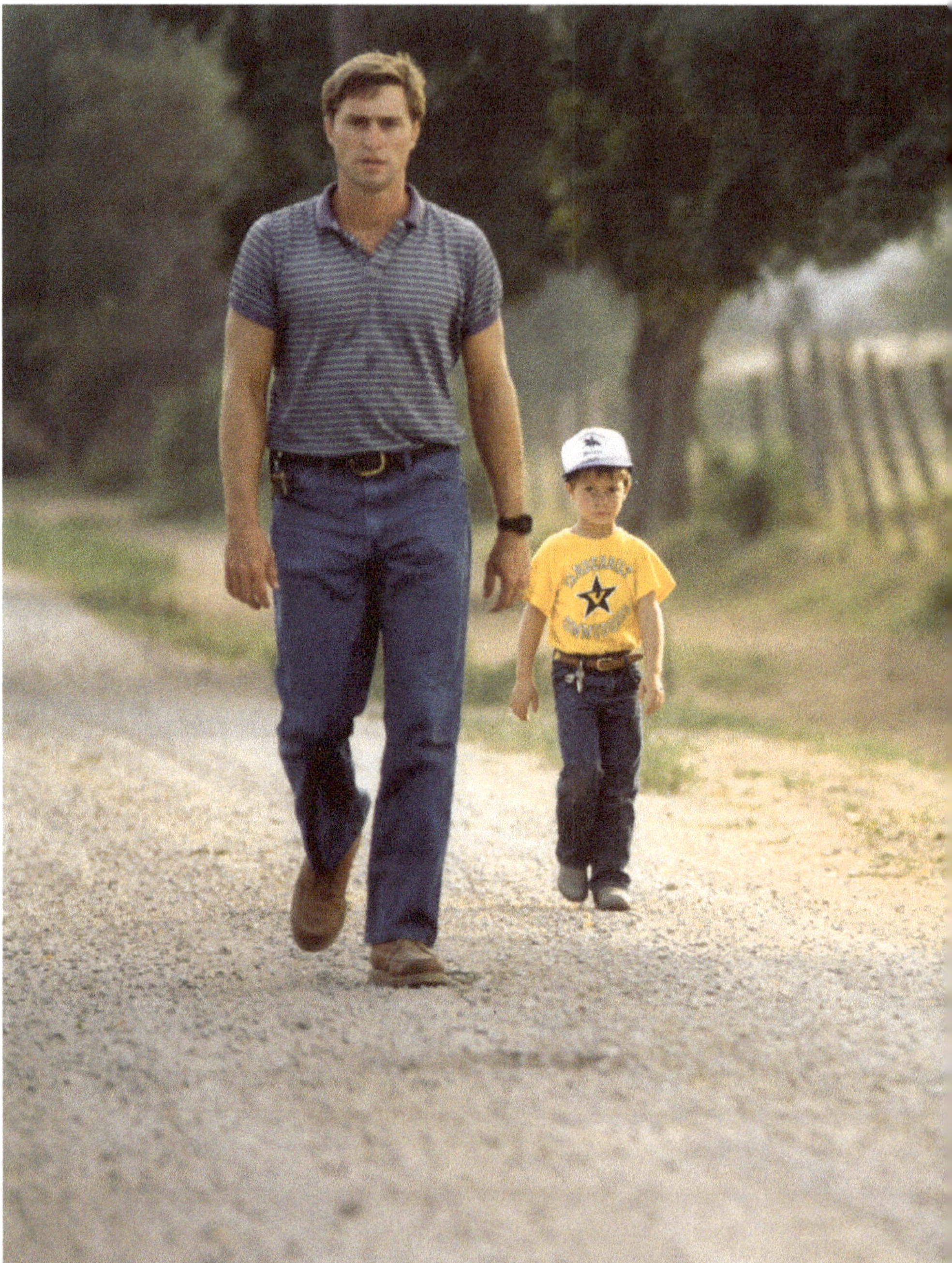

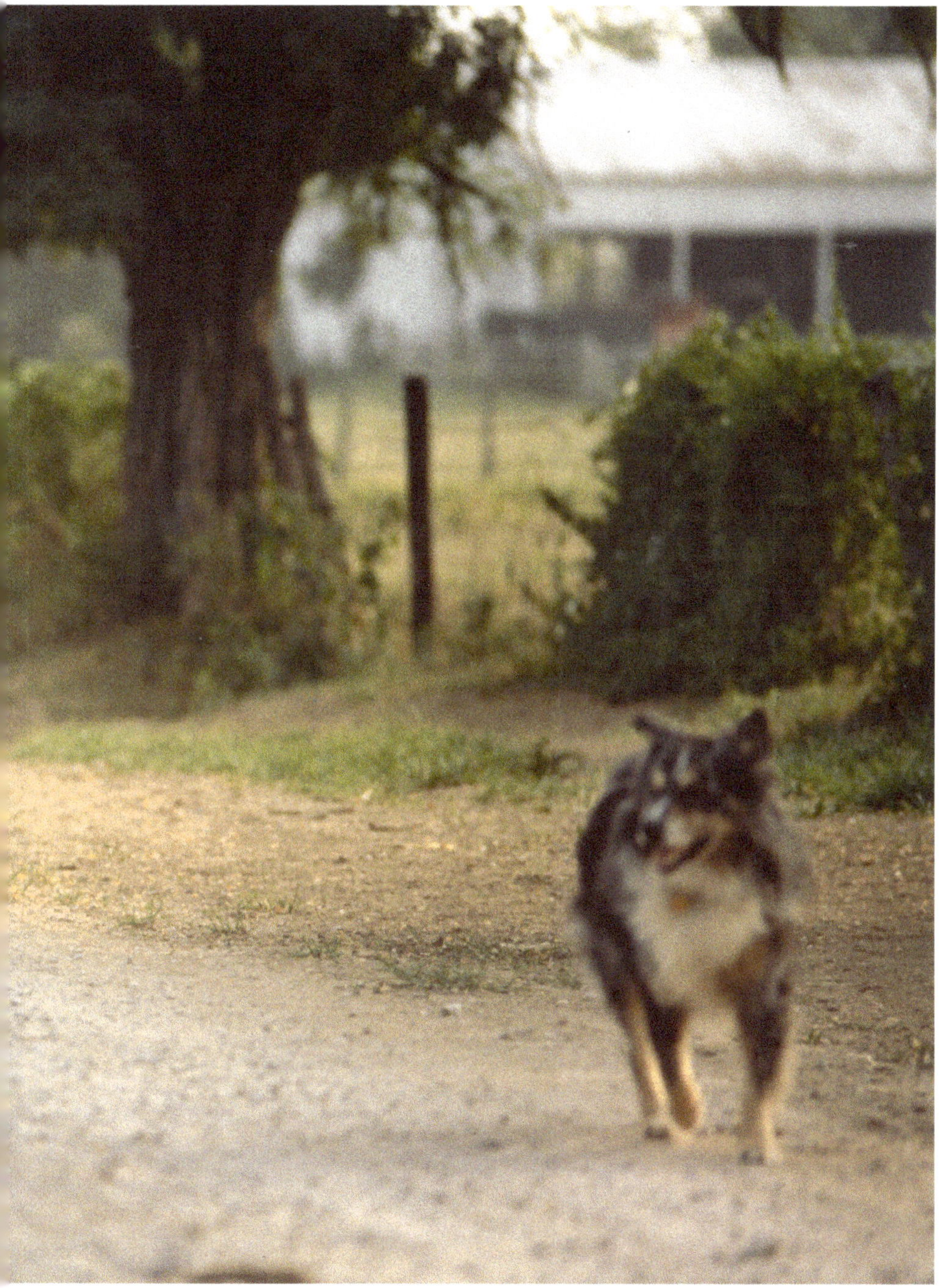

Sixth Annual
Spring Hill Lions Club Horse Show

Harlinsdale Farm's
PRIDE'S GENIUS presents...

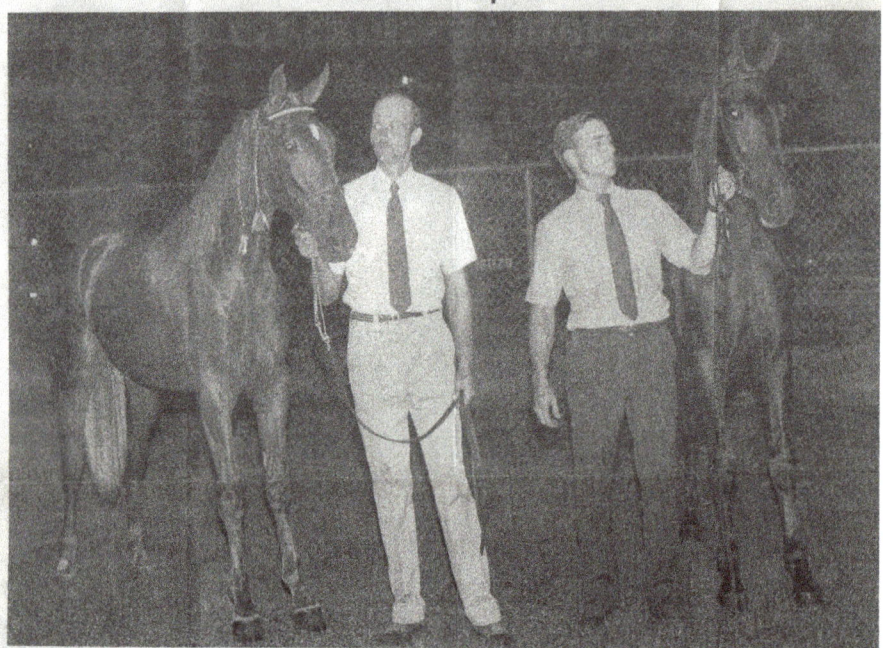

DAZZLING FOOTWORK and SPARK OF GENIUS

and Rocky Jones
Yearling Filly Champion
Owned By:
Rocky Jones
Spring Hill, Tennessee

and Clay Harlin
Yearling Reserve Grand Champion
Yearling Colt Reserve Champion
Owned By:
**Billy Sparkman &
Harlinsdale Farm**
Columbia and Franklin, Tennessee

Handled By:
Rocky Jones and Clay Harlin
Harlinsdale Farm
Franklin, Tennessee

Two winning consignments of the "Sellebration Sale."
Catch DAZZLING FOOTWORK, Saturday, September 3, selling as #180...
...and SPARK OF GENIUS, Friday, September 2, #142 in the sale catalog.

Sellebration Sale Boasts Top Five Average Of $10,730; Overall Average Of $3100

"It has to have been one of the best sales in our seven year history and in the 25 year history of Harlinsdale Farms," said Connie Bobo, secretary for C. A. Bobo and Sons' Sellebration Sale. "The averages are very impressive, with the top five being $10,730; the top 10 $8965; and the overall average for the 94 colts sold being $3100."

The sale's top selling entry was a powerful young stallion named PRIDE'S JOHN GREY. The Harlinsdale Farms consignment commanded a bid of $13,600 from Hoyte and Jane Eakes of Donelson, Tennessee, during the three day, August 27-29, Shelbyville, Tn., based sale. This fine prospect has been placed in training with Joe and Judy Martin.

Wayne Abee of Valdese, North Carolina, bought the sale's second highest priced colt in the $10,800 PRIDE'S ROYAL SON. This was a consignment from Billy Maddox. The number three colt belonged to Jack Ham, as he purchased PRIDE'S AVENGER C. H. from Clay Harlin for $10,250.

All of the top 10 selling colts in the Sellebration Sale were sired by PRIDE OF MIDNIGHT, in this sale which also features the get of SUN'S DARK BEAM and MIDNIGHT ALLEN. Other entries selling in the top spots were (4) PRIDE'S NIGHT BEAM, sold to Gordon Conrad of Kalispell, Montana, by Harlinsdale Farms for $10,000; (5) PEERLESS PRIDE, sold to Ron Inman and Claude Crowley of Salem and St. Louis, Missouri, by A. E. McEwen and Harlinsdale Farms for $9,000; (6) GENERATOR'S SISTER, sold to James C. Sullivan of Athens, Tn., by Harlin Hayes for $8100; (7) PRIDE'S PREMIER, sold to Wayne Abee by Billy Maddox for $7600; (8) PRIDE'S JET STREAM, sold to Joe Martin of Shelbyville, Tn. by J. W. Meek for $7000; (9) PRIDE'S BLACK KNIGHT, sold to Gary Cook of Cummings, Georgia, by J. W. Cross III for $6800; and (10) PRIDE'S TOP MAN, sold to Ross Summitt by Harlin Hayes for $6500.

A special consignment of broodmares started off the sale Wednesday morning. Margaret Holton's TRIPLE THREAT'S ROSE (the dam of World Grand Champion Three-Year-Old PRIDE'S SECRET THREAT) sold to Julia C. West of Kingsport, Tn. for $5750. This mare is in foal to PRIDE'S GOLD COIN. The feature attraction Wednesday morning was the special exhibition of the two new stars of the Harlinsdale Farms breeding lineup, PRIDE'S GOLD COIN and PRIDE'S FASHION. They attracted a tremendous amount of attention.

Dr. Warner Fusselle opened the sale to capacity crowds each day with a stirring address. Other sale officials included auctioneers Charles Yount, Ray Bennett, and Col. Fulton Beasley; ringmen C. A. Bobo, Eary Gregg, H. A. McArthur, Frank Bobo, and Bill Doak; and clerks Connie and Sandra Bobo and Martha Doak. Harlin Hayes read pedigrees at each of the three installments of the sale.

Jack Harn (left) joins Clay Harlin with PRIDE'S AVENGER C.H.

From left to right, Rocky Jones of Harlinsdale Farms, Joe Martin, Hoyte Eakes, and Judy Martin join PRIDE'S JOHN GREY.

The Harlinsdale Crew at the yearling auction, 1986.
Standing: Oscar Pruitt, Leroy Walker, Clay Harlin, Rocky Jones, Alfred Perkins
Kneeling: Tommy Edwards, Chris Ezell, Pat Ford, Dan Ford

Rocky parks out a yearling at The Sale, W. L. Holt assists, 1990.

Clay parks out a yearling, Bobo's Sellebration stables in the background, c. 1976.

Talbot rides Sunny the Pony in front of the Show Barn, 1984.

Clay teaches Talbot the finer points of rifle marksmanship, 1984.

Rocky and Debbie Jones, Linda and Dan Ford,
Johnny and Cathy Haffner, Faye and Clay Harlin, 2014.

Monty McInturff and Clay Harlin in front of the renovated Hayes House in 2024.
Monty is one of the leading fundraisers for the Friends of Franklin Parks, and has
been indispensable in his support for the preservation of Harlinsdale.

"Hey, I know you! Didn't we spend a night in jail together?"

-Dan Ford

Tyrannus Equus Rex

The reader is highly encouraged to skip this one. What follows is a story that must be told, but you don't have to read it. I can't in good conscious write a memoir about a horse-breeding farm and not talk about the process of breeding horses. I will do my best to use euphemisms and comical descriptions of events wherever possible in place of graphic illustrations. Young readers are advised to ask their parents for permission to continue.

Once all the mares were checked for their ovulation status and sorted for priority on the daily breeding schedule, the collection process could begin. This is where the aforementioned tag color and number conundrum gets a bit simpler because each color tag or neck tag corresponded to the desired sire chosen by the horse's owner. So, knowing the next stud horse in order of collection, Rocky or Dad needed only to call out numbers and we could fetch them from the fence or the barn and have them ready in the stockade for breeding. But I'm getting ahead of myself.

Before the breeding day got into full swing, all the equipment would be washed and prepped. Inside the breeding room was a closet in which hung an artificial vagina specific to each stud horse. This was literally a rubber bag the actual size of a horse vagina, with about a five-inch-wide opening at one end, narrowing at the other end to just the size of a twelve-ounce bottle (think of a baby bottle). To absolve me of the requirement to write "artificial vagina" twenty times in one story, this will henceforth be referred to as "the bag." This bag was double walled and the outer bag could be filled with warm water to simulate the body temperature of an authentic female horse. There were leather covers for the bags with a handle for someone to hold. Yeah, that's right; someone had to hold this bag while the stud horse mated with it. But again, I'm getting ahead of myself.

For a place that thrived on frugality, the breeding room was pretty impressive. Stainless steel counters and sinks lined the room and stainless steel buckets hung on the wall. Surgical soap and rolls of sterile cotton pads for washcloths were stacked in the closet. All the bags and bottles were washed with surgical soap every day and there was a hot water heater installed at some point before my time, so we had hot water to wash and clean. The sperm analyzer sat on one shelf, sterilized bottles waited on another, plastic gloves that covered from fingertip to shoulder ready to go in a dispenser on the wall.

Once the collection was complete, the sample was analyzed for the density and mobility of live sperm cells. So many million sperm cells per CC of volume collected, times total volume, divided by sperm cells required for reasonable success per mare, and thus how many mares we could breed that day. The sperm would then be transferred to the mare's uterus through a plastic tube guided to its target by Dad or Rocky's glove-covered arm. The mare would then wait the required number of days to be checked by Monty for pregnancy, and with a little luck, eleven months later she would birth a live foal. But I'm still not telling the whole story.

There's no use stalling any longer, so here we go.

It's not too late to skip to the next chapter.

Last chance.

Before the next stallion was brought to the barn, his personal bag would be filled with warm water to his desired specifications. Now, I never had any actual part to play in this. Knowing the exact temperature and desired firmness preferred by each stud horse was something way above my pay grade. Some of the studs in our barn would literally try and breed a fifty-pound bag of grain in a wheelbarrow. Others would need everything to be just right. Not too many distractions, a mare that played just a little hard to get, don't rush him, let him take his time, and then maybe the mare will get impatient and try to kick him once or twice, and finally he's ready to go. All this hard work and patience could be ruined if the bag weren't just right for such a discerning lover. What I'm trying to say is, Rocky actually knew just how these stud horses liked it and would fix up their bag just so to create the desired ambiance.

Just like the teasing stud Dee-Bo, the collection process required a teasing mare. This mare had to be sturdy and capable of bearing the weight of a stud horse in full mating ritual. A stud horse who wants to mate is no match for a mare who definitely does not, so she also needed to be in the mood for love herself. There seemed to usually be one among the breeding mares on any given day that fit this description, but on occasion a less-than-willing partner might need to be chosen.

This would work for some of the more masochistic studs who actually like to be kicked and brayed at during the process, but some of the more gentle lovers would need to woo her over.

In any event, this mare would be selected and taken to the hallway opposite the breeding room from the stockade to wait for her prince charming. Before anyone starts to formulate accusations of equine sexual assault in their mind—spoiler alert—the stallion doesn't actually mate with the mare. One might say the cruelest part of this charade is really the joke that gets played on him.

Now, think back to the original Jurassic Park movie. The SUVs get stuck just outside the T-Rex enclosure in the rain storm, the power is out, the protective electric fence is down, the suspense is building…and then the T-Rex,

"BRRAAAAAAWWWWAAAAAARRRR!!!"

With the nasal roaring sound of a thousand war trumpets as from some barbarian hoard. If you remember this sound then you have some idea of what a stud horse sounds like rounding the corner of the Show Barn with nothing but daylight between him and a mare in heat. I can picture W. L. (*Dubya-El*) holding a leather lead line at maximum arms-length to avoid getting pawed or stomped, stud chain over the horse's nose, mouth agape, nostrils flaring, his rear end fishtailing out as if maybe he could walk his business end to the barn all on its own and just leave his head behind, stud chain be damned.

And now I get to the point of this story. The war trumpet sounding from an inbound stud horse meant that someone was about to be chosen for a very important job. We had gone to all the trouble to sterilize each piece of equipment involved in the process from collection to insemination, save only one.

Out from the breeding room would come two stainless steel buckets: one filled with surgical soap and warm water, and one with warm rinse water. Each would also be filled with wads of sterile cotton for washcloths and two plastic, arm-length gloves tied to the handle of one bucket.

"Talbot, Head Man." I was chosen.

On went the gloves and with a bucket in each hand I went out to take my post. Now most readers might have seen a male horse at a horse race on TV, or perhaps on a visit to a farm once or twice. Some might have been curious enough to take a peek under the hood on the chance the animal needed to relieve himself. What you see during such an event is about fifteen percent of what this monster is capable of achieving.

Approaching down the gravel road from the Show Barn was something like a war mace being wielded by a sinister medieval knight in black armor. This beast was about three feet long and six inches in circumference with a comically large head on it like a toilet plunger. As the stud fishtailed his rear end out to try to escape from the hold W. L. had on him, this war club went swinging from side to side and smashed into his withers like a big league slugger knocking the dirt from his cleats before taking the plate.

These stud horses didn't need a calendar or a clock to know it was breeding time. They had probably been in their stalls swinging this cudgel around all day, smacking it into the dirty sides of their stall, stomping in manure piles as it dangled around their knees. In short, it was filthy and it had to be cleaned. That's where the "Head Man" came in. Someone had to actually get under there and catch this monster that didn't want to be caught—or maybe he did want you to catch it, which was actually way worse to consider—and clean it off.

I don't know why (okay, maybe I do), but everyone always watched this part. Most people would go back to what they were doing for the actual collection itself, but this always attracted an audience. It was part the possibility of watching a disaster, and part knowing exactly what the Head Man was going through. You were watching someone mentally force himself past the immediate danger of being stomped to death, the revulsion of grabbing onto this horrible thing, and then realizing he was on the horns of a dilemma with no choice but to press on and get it over with. It was a complex, emotional experience and we could all sympathize. Of course, that didn't stop any spectators from throwing verbal spears at the Head Man.

I assume if this same procedure were carried out at a veterinary clinic or some teaching hospital you would find nothing but straight faces and professional eyes hidden just behind clipboards with disinterested looks as if nothing-to-see-here. That's not how it worked at Harlinsdale. No matter how many times this process was repeated, the jokes never seemed to get old. I don't need to spell it out; you can make up your own. They are literally endless. But needless to say, the Head Man would have to block out the needling coming from the crowd and focus on the task at hand.

Rinse bucket staged far enough away so as not to be kicked over by the beast, soapy bucket in right hand, you'd confidently approach from the front left quarter.

"BRRAAAAAAWWWAAAAARRRR!!!"

Don't mess around; don't hesitate.
Reach under there and grab that sumbitch.

"Awww, he's really a nice boy. He don't mean any of that."

Ignore that; focus.
Hold onto the monster; grab a wad of soapy cotton and get to work.

"Awww Talbot; see, he likes you!"

Alright, that was pretty funny. Now focus. Next wad of cotton.
Wash; don't think about it; get it over with.
Alright, quick—grab the rinse bucket.

"Are you washin' it or playin' with it?"

Stop giggling. Focus. Don't let go of the beast!
You'll never get it back if you drop it!
No need to save water; grab a big wad of cotton and rinse it off.

"C'mon now; save something for Rocky."

Classic. One more check. No more soap that I can see.
Okay, done. Grab both buckets and get out of here.

It amazes me to this day that no one ever got hurt doing this. The first time I saw it done was like watching a lion tamer stick his head into a lion's gaping jaws. I thought for sure I was about to see what it looked like when a human head got kicked in by a horse. The man holding the stallion had a lot to do with this, holding his head high so he couldn't bite at you and keeping him squared up on all four legs so he couldn't kick out.

There's a sort of safe zone just behind a horse's forelegs so long as you stay far enough forward to be out of range of his deadly hind legs. Staying close enough to his side to touch him was better, in fact, kind of like a grappler getting in close to an opponent who prefers to strike, but even then it took a great deal of trust. I guess it was all about the angle of approach and reaction time, but it always worked out for the Head Man.

I think the rest of the process is self-explanatory. The poor stud got redirected into the bag and never knew the difference. The poor mare was left wondering if fate had landed her at a farm full of the dumbest stud horses on the planet who couldn't figure out how to properly procreate.

The breeding day went on; the Head Man went back to his post next to the stockade, hoping the ratio of farmhands to studs that day meant he only had to take one round in the arena. It was certainly a thankless job, and you could only break even. You were just as likely to pull extra Head Man duty whether you did it well or poorly. It wasn't some sort of stepping stone for promotion, simply a rite of passage. I count anyone who took a turn as the Head Man at Harlinsdale Farm among my brothers, and they are welcome at my campfire anytime[1].

---

1 If you don't get this reference, you still haven't seen *The Man From Snowy River* and you're letting yourself down.

Rocky tries to waive off any attempts at being photographed. He is holding "the bag" in his left hand, Clay and Leeroy stand by to assist in a "collection", c. 1980s.

"Yep, he's a Harlin."

–Rocky Jones

(Upon seeing me lose my temper on a particularly difficult yearling)

The Dance

This is what it was all about; the reason for it all.

They'd been there all summer, males and females kept in separate fields, but until now they were out of mind except during feeding time. They were still in their own worlds, virtually wild. In the winter, shortly after they were weaned, they had been worked for a few weeks in the hallway of the barn and maybe a few times out in the open on a lunge line. They knew the feel of a halter on their heads and had learned in some way to work with a human. As weanlings, they were only about a third the size of their future selves and to some degree you could still overpower them.

If you could catch them, that is. But once in hand, a grown man or a determined teenage boy could dig in his heels and the six-month-old would have to submit to the lunge line and halter around its head. I'm sure this experience went a long way to imprint on them that we were stronger and more powerful, and when they were weanlings this was true, but that was no longer the case. If they remembered anything from that first winter it was probably that they didn't like being caught. Being free out in the pasture was much better.

No one has more opinions about the proper care, feeding, and training of horses than someone who only has one horse. We were faced with breaking about seventy-five every summer. With one horse you can begin to imprint on it at an early age, teaching it as a foal to trust people, wear a halter, work on a lead line, never leaving them to the more natural process of growing up in a herd. After the few weeks we had with them in late November, we turned them out to learn their place in the world as a horse should. "You gotta let 'em learn to be a horse," I can hear Dad say, probably quoting Mr. Hayes. On some level this was beneficial because if kept separated they could each become the alpha in their own mind, whereas in a herd they tended to get put back in their place rather quickly. On the other hand, there were a few actual alphas out there and they came out of the process even more obstinate.

The socializing effects of the herd aside, the truth is there was just too much work to do and never enough people to do it, so mostly out of necessity they spent their second six months of life on their own. Sometime around early July we had to lay hands on these feral beasts again and by late August have them ready for prime time. Never knowing the world beyond a few hundred acres at Harlinsdale even existed, they would travel with us to Shelbyville and find themselves on display in front of a crowd of hundreds of people—most of them oblivious to the thin margin of control we had on these horses, children running around playing and screaming, tractors and trucks and trailers, horse show announcer or an auctioneer's voice blaring over a loudspeaker. And they had to look good. They had to have their shock and fear under control and somehow stay relaxed enough to show their natural gait and true potential.

Averaging around a thousand pounds and standing about fifteen hands high (five feet from hoof to shoulder), when we first brought them into the catch pen they would have a shaggy sun-kissed coat, a mane and tail tangled with burrs and twigs from the pasture, and the wild-eyed look of a trapped animal. Churning up a dust storm as they all pressed through the scrum of other yearlings to get as far away from anything on two legs as possible, and then finally throwing themselves at the wooden slats of the fence that blocked their escape. One by one we had to catch each of these colts and walk them in hand to their new stalls.

Some were submissive by nature once they were cornered; others would have to be cut out and run into a smaller side of the corral where we could close a large gate up against them, pinning them longways against the fence and wrestling halters onto their heads. Now the fight was just beginning. That first fifty yards or so from the catch pen to the barn might take twenty-five minutes of spinning, kicking, raring, and biting. This was no place for boys, and it wasn't until I had a few summers under my belt and about another forty pounds on my skinny bones that I was asked to grab a rope and join in the rodeo that first day. Dad still talks about the anxiety of this day every year, the anticipation of what was coming making it impossible to sleep the night before.

Like nearly everything else at Harlinsdale in my experience, no one ever told you how to do anything before you did it, at least not in the sense that there was some sort of school circle, "Let's all gather 'round and watch Cousin Bill demonstrate the proper way to halter a horse" period of instruction. You were expected to watch and learn, and if you didn't the result would be self-correcting.

For instance, to lead an unbroken colt, keep your elbow rigid and your shoulder pressed to theirs, or have them shy away from something on their far side (like a terrifying stick or a killer plastic bag) and trample over the top of you. Always keep your rope carefully coiled with no knots or tangles, or have a colt turn in on you and not have enough slack to give without getting pawed by a front hoof. Always send a colt into the stall in front of you, giving them slack on the rope and standing outside as you encourage them on in. Or you could try and lead them in shoulder to shoulder and get slammed up against the stall door that's just not quite wide enough for the two of you.

If a colt bolts on you, give him slack little by little as you work your way out to his side to get an angle on him, or try and hold your ground and find out just how powerful that animal really is. The truth is, if they wanted to make a break for it out in the open, there was essentially nothing you could do about it. It was better to let them have the rope rather than try to fight it out and end up "land skiing" for a few dozen yards before getting slammed flat on your face. You're gonna end up with a loose colt either way, so you might as well keep the skin on your hands and your dignity intact.

The male yearlings were put up in stalls down (up) at Oscar's Barn, while the females were put up in stalls around the main barns. Just like horse color, or the names of barns, or anything else at Harlinsdale, you could use three different words to talk about anything. Technically they were all yearlings, each being between one and two years old. A colt, again technically speaking, was a male yearling. However, it was just as likely that someone would refer to our entire stock of yearlings generally as "colts." Therefore, you couldn't just say "colt" if you were specifically talking about a male yearling, so people would say "stud colt."

A female yearling could appropriately be called a "filly" but would just as likely be called a "mare," or if she were especially ornery the derogatory "heifer," or worse. Given that any horse in its second full year of life was designated a yearling, some of our more talented mares would be bred in the fall; therefore, their offspring would be almost two years old by late August, making them more mature and considerably larger. These would be referred to as "fall colts," again irrespective of their sex. No one ever said, "fall filly." Getting a straight answer out of any good country person was nearly impossible, and this was no different.

If you got into an airplane and flew low over Harlinsdale anytime between July and August, you'd see sets of large rings out in open fields, as though a group of aliens had landed in flying saucers but hadn't quite mastered the art of flying in formation and left a catawampus set of crop circles behind. These rings were really the stomped-down earth left behind by dozens of colts working in circles at the end of a lunge line.

A round pen would be another way to do a similar training program but we never had any, at least not in my lifetime. In any event, the fields where we worked colts were multi purposed and we'd never use precious space with round pens that would have to be repaired, painted, and then sit idle for nine months of the year. Not to mention we'd have needed eight or ten of them to get the job done.

Once the breeding season wound down around mid-July, we worked every single colt every day. With maybe eight people working colts on any given day, each colt would get about an hour of work Monday through Friday. A few special cases might get some extra attention on the half day we worked Saturday. If we were going to a show that Friday or Saturday night, then each showman would be tied up with a single colt all day, but that's another story.

I loved working colts, it was the best of all the elements of Harlinsdale—challenging and sometimes dangerous, dullness and repetition spiked by moments of wild excitement. Not to mention it was a fraternal atmosphere, everyone working about forty to fifty feet apart with plenty of time to talk and joke about pretty much everything there was to talk and joke about.

Just like parking spaces, or pitch forks, or lunge lines, there were no assigned lunge circles but everyone seemed to have their favorite spot and it was proper etiquette to figure this system out and adhere to it. One of the lunge circles outside each set of barns had a tall, eight-to-twelve-inch diameter post planted in the center and was reserved for the hardest of hard cases. This circle was generally left available for someone who had a colt that really wanted to find out how strong it was. Tying your end of the lunge line to this immovable post, the colt could pull all he wanted and not get anything for it except a nice coat of sweat.

After a few weeks, you got to know pretty much what was waiting behind each stall door. What you hoped for was a nice, little, fourteen-hand colt with gentle eyes full of intelligence and interest, weighing in at around eight hundred pounds. Maybe some apprehension, but not fear. The other end of the spectrum was a colt that would be trying to knock the barn down before you even opened the door. A sound louder than a shotgun blast would ring out as he kicked out at the stall door. Then a deeper concussive sound that you feel in your chest as he threw his entire weight against the back wall making the barn shiver. This was the sixteen-hand, twelve-hundred-pound version, sporting the wild-eyed sideways look of prey eyeing a predator. I won't name names, but you might have noticed someone taking a well-timed trip to the powder room if he thought this colt was next in the order and he had drawn the short straw.

Given that we all stayed on more or less the same cycle, we would all be putting up a worked colt and catching our next one about the same time. Someone stopping by the barn around that time and not knowing what he was walking into might have a fair amount of concern. Up and down the barn you'd hear colts pawing the doors, throwing their weight into the back wall of their stalls, braying and neighing for each other as if there were a lion prowling the aisle. This would be followed by,

"Heahhh Now! Quit that!"

"Whooooah, Bwoah"

"Come ooown now; Easy, Bwoah[1]"

If you ever heard the stall door close behind someone, it meant they were going all in to the back corner after a particularly hard-to-catch colt. It was somewhat of a faux pas to offer to help an experienced horseman, but it might be worth a glance inside to make sure he wasn't in trouble.

One way or another, we all got a rope on our next yearlings and sent them out ahead of us into the hallway of the barn. Some crept out one timid step at a time as if they were re-entering a strange world where up was down and the barn floor was now liquid instead of solid earth. Others would blast out of their stalls as though this sanctuary where they had been safe and dry, watered and fed for the last twenty-three hours, was suddenly about to destroy them.

Each colt would be tied to the sturdy corner post of its stall for a few minutes of grooming and a gentle but firm hand rub to desensitize him to the touch of a person. After the nervous energy the colts had built up, this was our chance to imprint on them that they were safe and that interactions with people could be pleasant. As the weeks went on we would push their comfort level by working our hands down to pick up their feet,

---

[1] The pronunciation of the word boy by adding a sort of "w" sound after the "b" and finishing the word as if your lips were stuck in an oval shape was a hallmark of Mr. Hayes' manner of speaking. As in everything else he did, people adopted his mannerisms as their own as if they carried some sort of power over horses.

back further on their belly toward their withers, and up and over their back to their far side. They were still growing and too young to be ridden, but it was sort of a standing challenge to see if you could get one to trust you enough, or if you were simply brave enough, to throw a leg over and sit up on them for a few moments.

From start to finish, the colts were attached to a lunge line. We never used a shorter lead line unless we were in the show ring. The lunge lines, at least the ones we used, were about thirty feet of round rope, cotton or nylon, and about a half inch in diameter. The true purpose of the lunge line was to allow the trainer to work a horse at the end of this rope in a circle, thus sending the colt around a large diameter track while the trainer made a much smaller circle in the center. The colt would end up pacing out several miles while you in the center only had to step out maybe a quarter of that distance. In my working years at Harlinsdale we just said "lunging," but some of the old hands like Dan Ford would have called this "line working."

The other value to a lunge line was found in your ability to give slack to a spooked colt without losing control. Sometimes all they needed was just some personal space to collect themselves. If they spooked and you had only a few feet to play with, as with a lead line, you would have to constantly step forward into them and only exacerbate the situation. Worst case, they could choose fight over flight and with only a short lead line you would be forced to choose between a hoof to the forehead or letting slip your line and have a loose colt. With a lunge line you could let them have a few feet, maybe a dozen feet, without even so much as a lean in their direction. Once they had some space to calm down, you could start the dance again.

Tied to the wall, some colts suddenly would panic and want to rip the barn down[2]. This was especially true the first time they were tied up. During the first few days of working colts it wasn't out of the ordinary to see a few laid out on the floor of the barn, sitting on their haunches like a dog, heads held vertical by the unyielding lunge line tied to the barn wall, still convinced that one more determined thrashing and that barn would come apart and they could escape.

Once they had finally given up, had finished "having a come-apart" as Dad would say, all that was needed was to pull loose the safety knot on their lunge line and give them a few feet of slack to stand up and collect themselves. After this tantrum you generally had come to an understanding of one another—you weren't there to hurt them, and whatever was on the other end of that rope was a force they had to surrender to—eventually, anyway.

Grooming complete, we all headed out to the field to work our colts. Early on we kept to the small paddocks just outside the main barns. This was never explicitly stated; I just followed the crowd to where they had decided to work colts, but I imagine it was done in case one got loose. If one got away, at least we could keep them together in a smaller enclosure rather than see them tear out across a fifty-acre field trailing thirty feet of rope. Later on in the summer, once we were more confident in one another, we would move out to the larger fields and spread out a bit more. Or maybe it was done to give the field beside the Show Barn a chance to recover from the constant trampling. I never asked.

Humans project some sort of force that a horse can sense, farther than your physical presence, probably the amount of

---

[2] It is a testament to the solid construction of the Show Barn that we rarely, if ever, had to repair the posts that formed the corner of each stall. I've seen many colts try to tear one loose and all of them failed.

ground they imagine you can cover before they could react and escape your reach. Once you were at your circle, a properly-handled colt would be made to stand and face you, "parking out" with his legs squared off fore and aft, and then you could work out to his left, your right, and backward on his body, pushing him forward with this invisible force. Giving him more and more slack as he picked up his pace, you would continue to walk toward him just behind his flanks, gently urging him forward into an ever-larger circle.

Untrained colts would of course bolt, thinking they had found freedom once more. Holding back the slack on the rope and pulling their heads firmly toward you with your left hand as you continued to angle to your right toward their rear end, the colt would be worked into a never-ending circular track. Keeping a near-perpendicular angle between your rope hand and their heads was the key. If you gave them too much freedom with their heads and they got too much of an angle on you by turning away, it was pretty much over. You were going land skiing. If they spun their heads into you and you left too much slack in your rope, they could rare up and step over the rope, tangling it around their fore legs—in which case you'd have to drop it or risk injuring a leg or burning them with the rope as they tried to run.

Even trained colts, once they felt your hand go loose on their halters, would feel all the pent-up energy they had been holding back and take off in a bucking and kicking gallop around the circle. Anyone who ever took a turn working colts at Harlinsdale knows this feeling. It is at once exhilarating and frightening. You know you only have a thin margin of control remaining and everyone is watching to see if you can hold on. Giving out all the slack you dare until you have to start bearing down, you dig in your heels and sit back on your haunches to wait for him to hit the end of that rope. You feel your left arm fly out, hoping you can keep it flexed just enough to ease the shock as it reaches its limit, the rope burning in your hand as a few inches more rip through your fingers while you try and hold on.

Giving just a few more feet as you stumble forward, trying not to lose your balance, you gain some ground from the colt as he bends his neck back toward you. His rear end fishtailing out and away, now you have to quickly recover your feet and work toward him just enough to keep him moving forward. You're not even in your circle anymore, somewhere out in no man's land, but you have to keep moving forward. The guys working in the adjacent spots already pulled their colts in to get out of your way and watch the show.

Take up slack when he gives it, keep your rope coiled in case he bolts again. Work him slowly back toward where you started by squaring off part of his track. Finally you settle into the worked-down grass and dirt of an established lunge circle, the tension on your rope hand starts to subside. One by one you dare to relax your fingers and feel them burn and sting from the rush of blood back into them.

I truly wish I could go there now, coil up my lunge line and run my hand gently but firmly along my colt's neck from shoulder to jaw, then down across his cheek to take the halter in hand.

Strong forearm against his neck to keep him steady, let him know I'm still there, a gentle flick of my coiled rope against his flank to move him forward and head out to the field in front of the Long Barn.

If I had a time machine for the day, shortly after I sat down with Thomas Jackson before he stepped off on the flank march around Hooker's right at Chancellorsville, I'd drop in on Harlinsdale Farm at about 9:00 a.m. on a July Monday in the summer of 1998. I'd find an open spot right next to Rocky just so I could talk to him again, although you didn't just talk to Rocky. You waited patiently and respected the silence until he wanted to talk. Sometimes nothing needed to be said, just his silent approval that he trusted you enough with your colt to work in peace and without correction. I'd work my colt in the stillness of the morning, take in the smell of that field, feel the cool air still hanging low around the grass, and try to forget for just one day that it all had to end.

Clay works a yearling on a lunge line at the yearling auction, c. 1990.

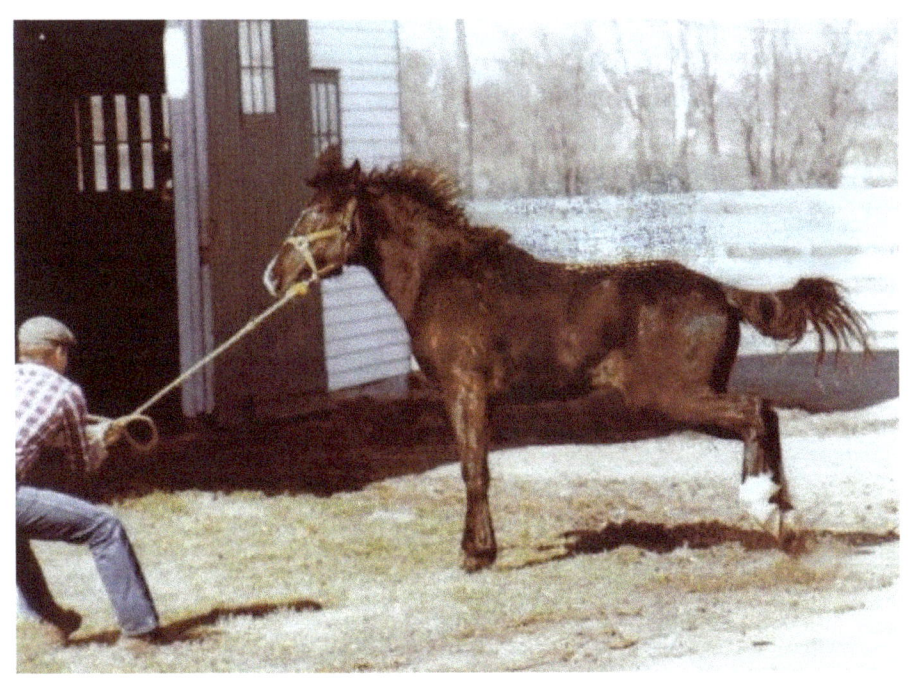

Clay digs in his heels to keep control of a spirited yearling, c. 1981.

"Catawampus crop circles" visible to the left of the Show Barn.

Alfred works Prides Gold Coin on a lunge line, c. 1990.

Clay has a "look here now" moment with a yearling, c.1990.

Rocky works a yearling colt down at the Upper Barn, c. 1980s.

Leeroy has a colt that "can't get right" spin around on him. He is trying to recover without having to drop the rope that is wrapped around the colt's hind end, c. 1980s.

Can't Get Right

It was a late July afternoon in 1982, a Tuesday, which meant a couple of things around Harlinsdale Farm. First and foremost, it was hot. The thermometer read ninety-five degrees but with the humidity that day the heat index must have been well over a hundred. It was also only a few weeks until the yearling auction in August, which meant the men of Harlinsdale had to make every day count. The breeding season was over and every day now focused on working each and every yearling for at least an hour. You weren't going to win with them every day; the name of the game was repetition and conditioning.

The time for picking fights was over; most of the colts had figured out the routine and were ready to work. There were always a few hard heads that were just too mean or unintelligent to realize their lives would be infinitely easier if they would just go along with the program. Then there was another group, a small few that had it all figured it out but were too smart for their own good. These were hard not to love because of their obvious intelligence and personality, but like a precocious child they would test every limit of your patience.

I say "picking a fight" because it truly was a choice. You could choose to keep your cool, stay patient and calm, and let the oppressive heat wear an ornery colt down over time. It might take every bit of that hour, maybe even every day for a week, but eventually they all forgot what they were fighting about and settled down. But there's something about having your arm repeatedly jerked nearly out of socket, your hands cramped and burned from the death grip you had to keep on the rope, the sweat dripping into your eyes and the ever present flies—sometimes they just got the better of you.

Sometimes you decided you'd just about had enough; today was the day. Right here, right now. And that's how Dad found himself sitting astride a wild-eyed bucking colt, the fence posts surrounding the upper barn whizzing past his right eye while Rocky called out encouragement from the end of a lunge line to his left, seriously regretting the sequence of events that had led him to his current predicament.

Throwing on a saddle and riding one was a last resort. They were still growing and a little too young to be thoroughly saddle broken, not yet ready to bear the weight of a rider for any length of time. But if nothing else was getting through to a colt, having a grown man throw a leg over and ride through every buck and kick and biting tantrum they could throw at him could turn the hardest of the hard cases into Sandy the backyard pony in one afternoon. This was a point of no return, however, and there was no backing down. Once the saddle went on, that colt had to be ridden.

We were not bronco busters; there was no round pen with high, smooth walls; no soft raked dirt on the floor of a riding arena to land on if you came off. If someone declared that a colt was going to be ridden or else, the else in that statement had a wide range of terrible outcomes, as Dad was about to find out. To make things worse—and I'm sure this thought was going through Dad's mind about as fast as those fence posts went whipping past—Dad hadn't even been the one to pick this fight. The original would-be bronco buster had lost his nerve and Dad had to step in and man up—which was worth noting for posterity—but at that moment the point was moot.

While this was by far the most dangerous part of breaking colts, it was likewise a rare occurrence. I can only recall someone using this tactic once in any of the five summers I broke yearlings at Harlinsdale, and in that case it was Rocky on one of his own colts. We had plenty of other tricks we could play that involved much less risk to any of the two- or four-legged combatants.

The real excitement and physical danger usually centered around the very first day when we got them out of the field to halter them and put them up in their stalls. You were guaranteed to end that week with bruises on your arms and shoulders, a few toes probably broken or sprained from being stomped on, and some black and blue legs from failing to clear the path of a colt that was trying to come over the top of you.

In the early days of their training, we harnessed their natural instinct to run away in order to keep them moving forward. The pressure on their halter from your hand holding them just behind the nose kept them turning back into you. So long as you kept moving forward, while you might be going in circles, you could eventually get to where you wanted to go.

As time went on you could get a few forward steps to every circle back around, and then eventually lead them out to the field and turn them loose into a lunge circle where you would wear them out for thirty minutes or so and then try leading them by the halter again. The trouble came if they ever spun around and faced you. Any one of them could pull you right off your feet and if they every figured this out, they never forgot it.

That is, until you introduced some horsepower of your own in the form of an International 1066 tractor.

This isn't nearly as cruel as it may sound; it was actually quite comical and ingenious in my opinion. At some point before my time, we had a metal bar fashioned onto a three-point hitch that could be attached to the back end of the tractor. The top of this contraption was a long, round iron bar that sat parallel to the ground, about eight feet long and sporting four metal attachment points where you could tie up a colt. The bar could be raised or lowered to match the height of a colt's chin.

The first trick would be to run a lunge line through the attachment points and tie him up with about ten feet of slack. As the colt threw everything they had into trying to back away, a tactic that had worked countless times before, the horseman would keep his hand calmly on the rope as the tractor inched effortlessly forward. The effect was to give the colt the impression that you were suddenly the strongest man alive and could pull him around with your fingertips.

This trick usually solved most of the hard cases, but there were always a few who were not yet persuaded. These would then be tied up to a much shorter rope only a few feet from the back of the metal bar, often side by side with two or three of their best friends. This gang of outlaws would spend the afternoon walking behind the tractor all over the back field. After fighting it out for days with one of these can't-get-right colts, I must say it was very satisfying to see them utterly defeated by a six-ton tractor.

All the driver had to do was put it in low gear and let out the clutch, and the tractor would crawl along at only a few miles per hour. For the first few yards all four colts would dig in their heels, squat back on their haunches, and give it all they had. Their hooves would scrape along the ground and till up the field, moaning and grunting and thrashing their heads from side to side. Then one by one, at first only a few steps at a time, all sixteen legs would step out just as relaxed as the walking horses they were born to be.

When my dad was growing up, this trick was done on horseback—which is something I admit, I'm very sorry to have missed. I see visitors to the farm these days decked out in cowboy hats and cowboy boots and I must admit it amuses me. No one ever wore a cowboy hat around the farm and any cowboy boots were not likely to survive the first day, so this is about as cowboy as it got at Harlinsdale. Mr. Hayes and the other legendary horsemen of an earlier era would saddle up a couple of big, stout horses with western saddles, tie a particularly resistant colt to the saddle horn with a short line, and take off with him across the fields for hours. When they came back you could lead that colt around like a puppy. Our method may have been more efficient in terms of man hours, but the old breed certainly had a lot more fun.

These sorts of tricks would fix the dumb ones, the all brawn and no brains brawlers. The smart ones, however, were a different problem. The personality traits of these colts more closely resembled a clever dog than a horse, but a dog that could drag you across a field or crash its half-ton body through a wooden fence using you as the battering ram. These colts would outwardly show eagerness to work, all the while waiting for you to drop your guard so they could slack off. They would fake confusion, as though they just couldn't figure out how to walk in a circle around at the end of your line.

With a trough full of grain in front of them they could be oblivious to a swarm of flies, but on a lunge line they might be defeated by one stubborn fly that just wouldn't leave them alone. They would have to stop over and over again to shake it off, and then look confused as if they weren't sure what to do next. Sometimes they would just stop for no reason and drop down to roll in the dirt for a while, then stand up and look at you like they forgot you were there.

It was hard not to love them, seeing them cleverly work out a problem to get out of work. All horses can sense tension and fear in your body language, but these colts could actually sense apathy or complacence.

For example, let's say you go into a stall to catch one and he's standing there as calm and patient as can be. You match his demeanor and relax a little bit, grateful to have drawn the long straw for once. You clip the lunge line under his chin and send him out into the barn hallway, expecting him to turn back and face you in anticipation of being tied up and groomed before going to work, just like he does every day. But not today. This colt instead takes advantage of the relaxed atmosphere to embarrass you in front of everyone.

After clearing the stall door, he decides to spin to the right, instead of back toward you to the left, and wraps the rope around his rear end. Suddenly terrified of this rope that five seconds prior seemed like an unnecessary afterthought, he backs away in startled confusion, wrapping the rope around his legs. You have no choice now—and he knows this—but to drop the rope and let him go. The only other choice is to confidently walk right up to him and catch him by the halter, pretending nothing is wrong. But a colt like this knows better.

There's no use holding the rope anymore; putting any tension on it will just pull the loose coils of rope snaked around his legs into a knot. This could induce true panic and risk a serious injury to his legs. So, you admit defeat, you drop the rope, and he casually strolls right out of the barn to find the thickest patch of green grass. He might get four or five big pulls on the grass before you can untangle the rope from around his legs and lead him away, all the while absorbing taunts from your buddies back in the barn.

Or let's say it's getting late in the day; everyone is tired; your guard is down. You've finally drawn a filly that seems to know the program and she settles down into a nice pace around the lunge circle. She's not pulling on you incessantly or trying to stop; she knows this behavior will only get correction from you and she's decided just to do her job—or so you think.

You decide that maybe walking in small circles inside of her big circle is a superfluous requirement for a filly like this, and you bet she'd probably just work herself and you can stand still for a minute and pass the rope around you from hand to hand. Since you've made it this easy on yourself, you might as well strike up a conversation with your buddy in the next circle. A few minutes later, the rope in your hand goes slack and the rhythm of waves coming down the rope from her bobbing head suddenly stop.

But she doesn't just stop; she feigns confusion as though maybe this were all part of your plan. Maybe you subconsciously gave her a little tug on the rope to tell her it was, in fact, time to stop. She dutifully walks directly toward you in anticipation of joining you for a little stroll while you lead her by the halter. Her face is lowered in gentle submission and her eyes look at you as if to say, "What a good girl I am today; you may pet me now."

You quickly pull in the slack to keep her from stepping over the rope and it startles her. All is not lost; it's actually kind of understandable that she'd be confused. You send a little flick of the rope in her direction, just a little gentle encouragement to get her going again, speaking gently you encourage her with a, "Come on now, girl; let's go." A little reminder to her that, while she is a good girl today, we still have work to do. But now her feelings are hurt; she's flustered and confused.

What do you want? You want me to change directions? Walk toward you? Back away? Make up your mind! I thought we were friends! Her eyes get wide and alert; her nostrils flare; she rears up. You panic, thinking she might catch a hoof over the slack in the rope and abruptly pull in all the slack. Now you've really done it; you scared her and now she's mad. You are not friends anymore. She shifts her weight and sits back on her haunches, backing away and throwing her head. You try out your best horse whisperer routine, "Whooooooaaaah now… eeeaaasssyyy, girl." She spins away and throws a kick in your direction. From an adjacent lunge circle you hear someone laughingly say what you already know—"She gone!"

Another trait that seemed to be absent in both the dumbest and smartest colts was trust. Don't get me wrong; there were plenty of scary things around Harlinsdale and it was easy to forgive a yearling for showing fear. Loud tractors, some sporting front-end loaders toting mountains of pine shavings high over their roaring engines, trucks and trailers with clanging metal doors bouncing along the gravel lane, to name a few.

My personal favorite was people with no horse etiquette visiting the Show Barn. Maybe we made it look easy, but that's probably because the uneducated spectators kept their eyes only on the horse. They never bothered to look at the intense concentration in the eyes of the horseman, the flexed shoulder ready to react in a split second to keep that colt from driving them into the barn wall. For some reason, like a toddler putting on her own shoes and perpetually choosing the wrong feet, these people would always approach a horse from the wrong side.

You always lead a yearling, or really any horse, from the left side. Whatever happens further to their left than your own body is of no concern to them. If you're doing your job correctly, you make it clear that the only thing they need to worry about to the left, in fact, is you. Anything to their right, however, is fair game. A loose feed sack, a scary snake-shaped stick, a tree blowing in the wind. All these things have been known to shape shift into dangerous panthers in the blink of an eye and horses are wise to treat them with serious concern. I can still feel the instant adrenalin shoot through my veins when a colt would startle at something, or someone.

The Show Barn was especially fraught with danger. It was always pretty dim in there, even in full daylight. We used its long hallway to hand walk the colts in never-ending laps to condition them to the show ring routine, and I'm lying if I didn't mention it got us out of the sun for a while.

About half way down on each side were two other short hallways, one being the marble entryway where we sat each morning and afternoon and also housed the two offices. The other held a concrete pad that served as a cross tie and housed a tack room on one side and something that could maybe be described as an equine pharmacy on the other.[1]

Visitors could never stop themselves from posting up on the edge of the marble entryway to admire the colts being paraded around the barn. Since we followed the American rules of the road at Harlinsdale, we worked in a counter clockwise pattern, thus placing the vulnerable right side of our colt toward the oblivious spectators. Adding further excitement to the experience, all the stalls on the south end of the barn held our stud horses.

---

[1] This room also housed the "cold drink machine," a novelty that was just about as impressive to me as a young boy as were the antique tractors/airplane cockpits in the Tractor Barn.

If it was dim in the hallway of the barn, it was downright dark in the stalls, especially after you and your colt's pupils had been thoroughly constricted from being out in the blazing sun. The stud horses would wait patiently in the dark until you were just abeam their stall door, and then they'd throw their massive bodies against its frame and let out the T-Rex roar. All you could see was one bloodshot eye pressed against the open slats of the stall and hear a rolling guttural chuckle coming from the darkness.

Once the colt's nerves were thoroughly frayed by walking this gauntlet, the final attack came just as you cleared the last stall before the marble entryway. Now fully alert, muscles as tense as a drum, the colt was practically walking on the tips of his hooves with his tail held straight out and nostrils flaring. All your shoulder strength was engaged in trying to keep this colt off you—and you had to lean in at about a twenty-degree angle to keep your balance. Just then, the spectators would initiate the ambush.

Practically invisible in the blinding light emanating from the open entryway, they would burst out, "Oooooh, boy; look at that one!" Bucking, kicking, rearing, trying everything in its power to run for the hills, your colt explodes right next to you. It didn't take too many experiences like this to teach you to do a little reconnaissance before taking a lap in the Show Barn. Any strange vehicles parked out front, especially one parked in an actual parking spot in front of the office, was clear indication of an impending ambush and thus grounds for an immediate retreat.

All of this was just part of the experience; it wasn't really the colt's fault. But as the summer wore on, there were a few standouts who became notorious. You could do the math and see that someone was going to draw a monster in the next round. This is where you might notice a horseman or two take a strangely timed trip to their truck or feel a sudden urge to use the men's room. I always tried to put on my best poker face and take what was coming to me, even welcoming the challenge as I got older; but all the while I was secretly hoping to hear over my shoulder, "Go on and get the next one, Talbot. That one's mine."

"ARE WE HAVING A GOOD TIME YET?"

-JOHNNY HAFFNER

(TO BE USED WHEN NO ONE WAS HAVING A GOOD TIME)

Clay's Gonna Be Alright

Well on that fateful Tuesday in 1982, Dad hadn't actually drawn the short straw. He was minding his own business and dutifully working his own colt out behind the Upper Barn. He would also prefer that the guilty culprit remain anonymous, so for the purposes of this story we'll call him Teddy. Teddy was just about as hot headed as the colt he had drawn that day and had everyone on edge with the amount of angst he and this colt were creating. He clearly didn't have the requisite patience that afternoon to get through a session with this yearling. Dad and Rocky were probably wishing they had just taken him instead of Teddy.

"Who's workin' who over there? Looks like he's getting just what he wants out of this deal," Rocky said.

"Oh, I'm doin' alright, but he ain't. He's about to get right, though. I'm gonna ride this sumbitch," Teddy declared.

Dad pleaded with him, "Oh come on now, we don't have time for that; don't start nothin' you can't finish."

Too late. Teddy was already pulling in his rope, the colt parked out facing him with nostrils flaring, eyes wide. Teddy snatched the halter under the colt's chin and led him fishtailing and prancing back to the barn. Dad had no choice; this was not a one-man effort. He pulled in his colt and followed Teddy into the barn. The trouble maker, the four-legged one at least, was tied up to the wall of the barn and left to stew for a bit as they gathered the tack needed to saddle him up. There was no need for a bridle; Dad would hold this colt with a halter and lunge line. One of the western saddles was chosen so the rider, ostensibly Teddy, could keep a better seat and hold onto the horn with his hands and pin his knees under the wide pommel.

Horses can make you think they have a tough hide and don't feel much pain, but at the same time they can feel a single fly land on their backs and twitch just the right muscle to shake it off. The sensation of a saddle pad and saddle on their back was altogether new and terrifying, not to mention the feel of the girth being tightened around their flanks. It took both men to hold the colt steady and keep the saddle in place while someone braved his underside to attach the girth.

Right about now I imagine Teddy was starting to get a sick feeling in the pit of his stomach. Dad and Rocky were probably doing the math to figure how many colts they would have to neglect that day and which ones they should prioritize with the time they had left, that is, after this charade was over.

With the saddle now installed, both men stepped back and let the colt get used to the feel of it. He was by no means ready to give up; instead he stared backward as far as the rope would allow at the new contraption attached to him. With nostrils flaring he proceeded to vacate his bladder and bowels, an instinct shared by all animals prior to a fight. If Teddy felt this same instinct, we'll never know, but I imagine he was battling the same urge himself. For now, he maintained his determination to see this thing through.

He slowly approached the colt and eased the weight of his left foot into the stirrup. Slowly and smoothly he shifted his entire weight into the saddle and found the other stirrup with his right leg. The colt thrashed and kicked, but being tied to the wall he didn't get very far. Teddy held fast to the saddle horn and kept his center of gravity low and forward over the colt's fore legs.

"You ready?" Dad asked.

"Yeah, I reckon…" answered Teddy, sounding unsure.

Dad eased the knot loose, collected the rope into coils in his left hand, and slowly eased the colt back from the wall. All the energy pent up in the yearling's 1,100-pound body exploded, and horse and rider quickly exited the barn. Dad fed out twenty feet or so of rope and kept pressure on the colt's halter to urge him into a circle. The colt was so preoccupied with trying to dislodge whatever evil force had attached itself to his back that for once he obeyed the tug on the lunge line and turned in toward Dad and began a bucking-and-kicking counter-clockwise circle at the end of the rope.

By Dad's account, Teddy managed to hold on for about sixty seconds, an admirable feat for sure; but it was not enough. He lost contact with the saddle on a particularly hard buck and came down square on the saddle horn with his crotch. On the next buck he threw his feet clear of the stirrups and swung his legs free of the saddle, landing on his feet but quickly dropping to his knees in agony.

Dad was sick in his spirit. Not for Teddy, though; he could have choked Teddy at this point. He knew what every horseman knows. Someone had to get back on that colt, and that someone was going to be him. Rocky pulled in the colt he had been working and tied him up in the barn. Rather than let the colt have time to process his successful first round, they determined to get right back to it.

Dad eased his weight onto the colt's back and sat up in the saddle, finding a good, solid seat and making sure to keep his heels low and his toes loose in the stirrups in the event he also needed to dismount. The colt again exploded into a bucking circle at the end of Rocky's line. Dad held on with everything he had, one hand on the saddle horn and the other gripping a fistful of the colt's mane. Round and round they went, Dad getting into a rhythm with the colt and thinking he might be just about to break him.

The paddock outside the upper barn was bordered by a wooden fence, with four-inch by four-inch wooden posts laid out every four feet. The ground itself was impossibly hard packed and littered with gravel and crumbling chert rock. It sloped in two directions toward the edges of the fence, and there was a large concrete water trough in the middle of one of the fence lines. Dad tried to put all these hazards out of his mind and focus on the positive trends he felt from the colt under him. He was getting worn out, starting to settle down. A few canters and then a few pacing strides were starting to find their way in between the bucks and kicks. The colt was throwing his head around a little less and starting to focus on his own breathing and exhaustion.

As Dad and his mount rounded the circle closest to the fence row at the eastern edge of the paddock, the lights went out. The last thing Dad remembers is the colt taking a stumble, his front end dropping toward the ground, and the colt throwing his head down to try to catch his balance.

Both horse and rider went down head over heels, and Dad's head found one of the four-inch-thick fence posts.

"THHHWHAAAAACK!"

Rocky said it sounded like a canon shot. The colt rolled over onto his feet and got up, but Dad lay motionless. Rocky truly thought Dad was dead.

Time is lost in Dad's memory of the next few hours. He remembers "coming to" in the hallway of the Upper Barn and seeing Rocky and Billy Maddox, a longtime customer and friend of Harlinsdale. He recalls them talking about him until suddenly the lights went back out. The next thing he saw was the view of Franklin's Five Points intersection from the bench seat of the farm truck, Rocky holding him upright with his right hand and driving with his left. They took him to the old hospital on West Main (which is now office space for Williamson County government services), where Dad remembers lying in an ER bed while nurses asked him his name, the names of his wife and children, our birthdays, the usual drill.

Around this time, the phone rang at our house in Franklin. Mom answered and heard a voice she did not expect. She had known Rocky for almost as long as she had known Dad, but Rocky had never called our house before, especially not when Dad was already at work. Hearing his voice on the other end of the line, she instantly knew something was terribly wrong. Rocky didn't exactly alleviate this concern, leading off with the ominous announcement,

"Faye, Clay's gonna be alright—He's conscious now."

There was no CT scan or MRI; these things were available at the time but not at our small-town hospital. They did an x-ray of his head—the next best thing they could offer—and identified a fracture on the right side. He obviously had a major concussion. In truth, he most likely had a brain hemorrhage. He suffered the effects of this injury for years, and possibly still to this day. He has struggled with migraines, memory loss, and depression throughout the intervening decades.

In today's world he would have been placed in a trauma unit for the first twenty-four hours or more, spent days in a neuro ICU, and then been discharged with strict instructions to avoid any unnecessary physical or mental activity. In the days and weeks that followed he would have been given more CT scans and monitored closely by a neurologist for any symptoms associated with a traumatic brain injury. As it was, he stayed in the hospital through Thursday and was discharged with instructions only to rest, avoid any pain meds, and for Mom to not allow him to sleep too long without being checked on.

There was something about belonging to Harlinsdale that left you sick thinking about someone else having to do your work. It was years into our childhood before Dad had the stomach to relent to Mom's demands that we take a family vacation in the summer. He couldn't imagine being able to enjoy himself all the while thinking about the guys back at the farm having to pick up the slack. Now he was being asked to lay in bed and rest? How could he face them again knowing they had been working extra colts in the heat for every day he lay around in the air conditioning? What would Henry Clay Harlin, or Wirt Harlin, or even worse—what would Harlin Hayes do?

Having all the stubbornness that eight generations of horsemen could ingrain in him and being thoroughly infected with the illogical work ethic of Harlinsdale Farm, Dad went back to work on Friday. That Friday night, he won the yearling stallion class at the Belfast horse show with a colt named Coin's Double Pride.

The Show

It's hard for me to put time stamps on the memories of those years. It all seems to have happened when I was the same age, but that of course, is not true. I was more or less fully functional as a farmhand by my third summer, when I was sixteen, but for that first year I was in some ways still a liability. I was probably only mildly trustworthy with even the most docile colts. I imagine the colts I worked that summer were handpicked to let me cut my teeth at horsemanship without getting hurt.

Even three or four years later when I could handle a colt with the best of them, there were still a few that everyone knew were designated as a "Rocky only" colt. He had a few special projects and you were never going to get him to let you have a turn with them. Dad wasn't quite as picky, but for at least a few summers he would let me off the hook and tell me to skip one every once in a while, leaving it to someone with more experience and lead in their boots.

The first evidence I have of taking a yearling to a horse show is from 1996, which would have been my second year at Harlinsdale. That summer, after my freshman year of high school, I was ready to take one to the show. Now, this wasn't The Show in Shelbyville, just "a show"—like Lewisburg or

Columbia. Or for instance, the Spring Hill Lions Club Horse Show. I still have the silver cup bearing that very inscription sitting on a side table in my living room, my trophy for a first-place finish in the yearling filly class. Any one of these smaller preliminary shows is where people came to show off what they were going to take to The Celebration in August. This was our chance, as well, to showcase our stock of yearlings and gain interest in our auction sale.

There were probably horse shows around middle Tennessee every weekend in the middle-to-late summer, but there was no way we could go to all of them. We might have gone to two, maybe three at the most; and we probably only managed to show two fillies and two colts at a show. Part of the problem was lack of interest on the part of many of the farmhands. You didn't get any overtime pay at Harlinsdale Farm, and spending a Friday or Saturday night doing what you did all day at work was not appealing to most.

For some it was worth it for the social aspect, running into old friends and walking horse people from around the area. For others, Rocky and Dad for instance, they had skin in the game because they personally owned a few mares and had some colts to sell that year and wanted to show them off. I can't say exactly what it was for me; it didn't seem like I had much choice. Not in the sense that I was forced to do it, but in the sense that it was the natural progression of my desire to become like them, accepted into the club of horsemen.

In any event, I was going to the show either way—my whole family was going just to enjoy a summer night out—and in my second year at Harlinsdale Farm, I'd be damned if I was going to another horse show as nothing but a spectator.

The other problem with trying to take yearlings to a horse show every weekend was the neglect it would render on the other seventy-some-odd yearlings that needed training. A colt that was selected for a show had to be worked all day by the showman, and I mean literally *all day*. When everyone else broke from the morning ritual to grab pitchforks and start throwing out stalls, you grabbed your lunge line and started grooming your colt. When everyone else finally made it out to the field to join you working a fresh colt, you were probably on hour three with yours. They would lunge for thirty minutes and then head off to hand walk their yearling for another fifteen minutes or so and take them to the wash rack—and you would still be there.

After lunch, you would go back and get that same colt out again, except now instead of the camaraderie of the lunge circles, you were headed out on a solitary walk for miles and miles, up and down the lane, in and out of tractors and trailers and barns, trying to desensitize your colt and put it to sleep on its feet. So for every farmhand that was going to the show, there were six or seven yearlings that wouldn't get worked that day.

I won that silver cup with a jet black fall colt (a filly in this case) named Show Sheen, but that wasn't my first show. Belfast, Tennessee was the place and I had a vivid image of the filly I took, but for the life of me I couldn't remember her name. I even tried to cheat and look it up online, but apparently the Belfast Lion's Club hasn't digitized any horse show results for posterity. I remembered she was a really pretty light chestnut filly, a Dark Spirit's Rebel filly out of a mare known for particularly spirited colts.

And then, as luck would have it, in the middle of working on this story my basement flooded. Cleaning out old boxes and seeing what could be salvaged, I came across a framed newspaper clipping my mother had saved for me. It was an advertisement for our annual yearling auction featuring "Rebel's Golden Girl," her eyes and ears transfixed on me as

I was presented with our blue ribbon in Belfast. She was just as pretty as I remembered.

I also remember that she wasn't my first choice. I had chosen another filly, a really gentle filly out of a mare everyone called Bonny, who reliably foaled the most docile colts year after year. A combination of nature and nurture, Bonny was a gentle and trusting horse and she instilled this trait in her colts both genetically and by her example.

While this was great for a nice break during the day—working a sleepy little eager-to-please filly instead of a colt trying to pull your arms out of socket for thirty minutes—this wasn't what you might look for in a show horse. If I were to pick out a filly to saddle break so my daughter could learn to ride, this was the horse. She was a darker chestnut, maybe bay though I can't quite remember, but I know she was on the smaller side like Bonny's colts always were.

I had chosen her not for success in the winner's circle but for general overall success, which I had defined as (1) not getting hurt and (2) not being embarrassed in the show ring by a misbehaving yearling. I'm not sure how long I kept up this fantasy that Rocky and Dad would let me take this dumpy little boring filly to a horse show just to have an easy time of it, but it was never going to be. I could tell they were patronizing me after a while but I tried to ignore it.

The show was on a Friday night, and one day leading up to it I was working a flashy little chestnut filly out in the field next to Rocky. She was prancing around the circle, her tail turned up as though she had so much anxiety that she couldn't contain it all in her body, nostrils flaring wide as she blew lungfuls of air out in a trumpet noise the way horses do when they are full of themselves.

She was one of the few that had it all figured out, always watching you with one eye while using the other to plot her escape if given half the chance. This was the kind of colt that gave you a shiver if you momentarily got a coil of rope tangled around your foot, knowing she'd drag you bouncing across that field and probably enjoy it.

Watching this filly move around the circle, Rocky asked,

"Talbot, you wanna win on Friday night?"

"Well, yeah," I lied.

This was something I hadn't really considered, winning that is. I just wanted to go and get it done inside the bounds of my aforementioned criteria for success.

"If you wanna win, you'll take that filly right there," he said.

"Her? No way; look at her."

Right about then she kicked out with both rear legs and took off in a bucking canter around the circle that jerked my left arm to its limit as I ran out of slack to give her.

"She'll win that filly class, and you'll be just fine. She'll trust you. You just gotta get her there."

If there was anyone I ever knew who was qualified to make a bold prediction like that, it was Rocky Jones. He probably knew before that filly was born that she was going to be a show horse. You could point at any single mare at Harlinsdale Farm and he could tell you off the top of his head her lineage, the sire of her current foal, the sire of her yearling, and what her colt would be like next year if she were bred to any particular stud in the barn. If I was willing to listen, Rocky was giving me some privileged information. He had his own colts to show, but if he was to pick any filly on the farm to win a yearling class, I currently had her at the end of my lunge line.

It's worth a moment of digression to explain just what it is that makes a Tennessee walking horse special, and what you might look for in a good show horse. So as to not open myself up to getting big-leagued by more knowledgeable horsemen, I'll keep this as simple as possible to get the point across. The basic natural gaits of a horse are the walk, trot, canter, and gallop.

Thoroughbreds, quarter horses, warmbloods, Arabians, and even feral mustangs will all naturally perform these four forward gaits. Tennessee walkers, however, do not trot[1].

Since I brought it up, the trot is a two-beat gait in which the legs work in diagonal pairs. Watched from the side, you might notice the left front and right hind work in tandem moving together, while the left hind and right front do the same. To say it another way, the legs on the same side work opposite each other, moving toward the horses middle together, and then moving apart toward the extreme front and back together.

This is great to keep a horse collected for tight turns or jumps, or to pass to the side in the diagonal. I wouldn't know it until I was in my early thirties, when my wife and I began to collect Thoroughbreds, but I had never really learned how to ride in the classical sense. Riding a horse through a trot requires balance and timing to "post" with the horse on every other beat, and the rider must choose which diagonal pair to post on depending on how you want your horse balanced. The rider needs to be very in tune with their mount and thinking ahead to what they will be asking of their horse and adjust their post accordingly. This requires a much higher level of effort and skill

---

1 I was "big-leagued" by Dr. Johnny Haffner himself during the proof phase of this book, and it is worth a footnote to be correct on this matter. Walking Horses actually can trot. Due to a gene they share with *standardbred* and *Icelandic* horses called the DMRT3, while it is possible for them to trot, they prefer to move in a lateral pacing gate. As Johnny recalls, my great grandfather Wirt was fond of saying, "No trot, no horse", to excuse a walking horse caught in a trot.

on the part of the rider. I'm sorry, walking horse people, but it's true.

That being said, if you want to go for a long ride and feel the power of a big horse driving up the ground beneath you, give me a Tennessee walking horse any day. The most unique thing about a walking horse is a gait known as the *running walk*. Unlike the aforementioned breeds, the walking horse is a "naturally gaited horse." Naturally because this unique gait does not have to be taught to a Tennessee walker; they will naturally perform it even as a yearling. If you watch a walking horse move from the side you will notice that they move their legs on the same side in tandem, as opposed to diagonal pairs. That is to say, they will step with their left front and left hind in short sequence, and then shift their weight to repeat the movement with their right front and right hind.

This motion is exaggerated from the flat walk into the running walk, where the horse will drive harder and harder with their rear end while pulling their fore legs farther and farther up and out of the way. Some gaited horses will break into a two-beat gait known as a *pace*, but a true walking horse will keep the smooth four-beat gait of a walk, even as they accelerate well past the speed of any other horse performing a trot. At a running walk the walking horse can travel at about twenty miles per hour with merely a side-to-side motion that the rider can sit through, and both horse and rider can cover a lot of ground without the fatigue of a traditional trot.

Now, since no one was riding any of our yearlings in a horse show, it actually took a more discerning eye to spot their future talent. Right out of the barn, they pretty much all looked the same, just balls of wound-up energy.

For the first ten minutes or so they were all tight like a spring and had to work it out for a while. Once they settled down, however, the natural rhythm of that smooth, flat walk would start to show itself. A more exaggerated head nod as they shifted their weight to pick up their front legs higher and stretch farther forward, a sort of hinge point in their back end like a German shepherd as they drove farther and farther forward with their rear legs.

If you kept an eye on the fall of their front hoof and marked that spot on the ground, you could see just how far past that mark they would step through with their back leg. A good colt might overstep their front hoof by a foot and a half. Add that to a colt with good conformation, pretty color, alert and intelligent eyes, and you might have yourself a show horse.

Well that could describe any number of the yearlings we bred in a given year, as my great-grandfather Wirt would have said, "We only have good, better, and best." The last part was something simply intangible, something that only a horseman like Rocky or Dad or Granddaddy could see at a glance. Some kind of mojo that would only show itself in the ring if you could bring it out of them.

So there I was, Friday afternoon on show day around nine hours into a fifteen-hour tribulation with Rebel's Golden Girl. At this point she was like a puppy on the end of a leash. Sleepily following me around everywhere, immune to the sights and sounds around her. By now I had taken her past loud tractors, made her stand still as trucks and clanging metal trailers drove past, walked her in and out of strange barns, across the old wooden bridge down the lane. She still had never actually been loaded on a trailer, or even seen anything of the world outside of Harlinsdale. She had probably never been around more than a dozen people at a time, and certainly had never seen big floodlights mounted on thirty-foot poles around a large grass arena surrounded by hundreds of them.

Before we went home to get ourselves cleaned up for the show, we bathed and groomed our colts. I'm doing pretty good to remember what I can about my own colt, so there's no way I can expect to remember anything about the others we took to Belfast that Friday night, but there were probably three or four. I imagine Dad and Rocky each showed one, and maybe Bill showed another. Like I said, I can't remember. In any event, the end of the work day was a team effort as all the non-participants pitched in to get our colts ready. We bathed and conditioned hair and brushed out manes and tails. Even the old flatbed Chevy and gooseneck trailer got a good bath and their tires shined. Each of the colts got a fresh trim with the electric clippers and had a ribbon braided into their forelock and carefully passed through a leather show halter. I didn't know it at the time, but learning to braid hair was a skill that has paid off all these years later, now that my wife and I have been blessed with two daughters.

Meanwhile, the Quaker value of simplicity ran strongly through the older generations of Harlins, and this was likewise strong in my grandfather. He was never one to show off, never one to exaggerate or draw attention to himself or his things. He always drove a sensible truck, and he would never buy a new piece of equipment if an old one could be fixed, no matter how much time was lost in repeatedly fixing it.

We were one of, if not the preeminent walking horse breeding farm in the industry, but we would take the same old flatbed truck to a horse show that we used to pull hay wagons. We had a pretty nice aluminum gooseneck trailer, but he would never pay the money to paint it up with even a simple logo, much less cover it in the iconic green and white colors of Harlinsdale Farm. We rode to the show sitting three or four across on the bench seat of a rust-colored Chevy 3500 dually, the man in the middle (me) having to contort his legs out of the way every time the driver needed to shift gears.

No matter how worn out they were, a ride in an open-air stock trailer to the show grounds would always wake up the colts. Every time we stopped at or started from a red light going through town, it sounded like opening day of dove season as the colts all kicked out at the sides of that aluminum trailer. Their sleepy, puppy dog eyes would be long gone by the time we unloaded them from the trailer. To some degree, the whole process of the day had to be repeated by walking them around, loosening them up, exposing them to the new and scary things they would see at the show.

At this point, you had both been literally walking all day and you still had a few hours left until it was show time. After all they had been through that day, the only constant in the experience was you, and now you had their complete trust. As it got closer, you'd give them another grooming session, fix any loose braids, reapply some Showsheen conditioner, touch up some hooves with black polish.

The showman's appearance had some value, but it wasn't really that significant in my opinion. Slacks, a dress shirt, maybe a tie, definitely no hat. Presentable but forgettable, not distracting was the general idea. It was always interesting to suddenly see some of the guys cleaned up and dressed up after only seeing them in work clothes my whole life. Rocky always wore a hat at work; I mean always. Which is why at horse shows it never failed to surprise me, even though I had known him my entire life, that Rocky was bald. Bald in a way that only a man who spent his entire life out in the sun without exposing the top of his perfectly white bald head could be.

Another thing that sometimes caught me off guard at horse shows was learning Rocky's real name wasn't Rocky—

it was actually Emery. Save only the occasional horse show announcer, I don't think I ever heard anyone call him that, not even his wife.

Show time. The showmen and their yearlings gathered around just outside the gate, waiting for the class to be called in. Most kept their colts moving in small circles to keep their anxiety low and their minds on their business. There wasn't much jockeying for position; there was usually enough room around the show ring to spread out and let the judge get a good look at each colt. At big shows, like the Futurity class at the Celebration, this was not the case. You would cut each other out if you had to or take it wide into the corner to find a nice gap for the straightaway pass in front of each judge. The 1996 Belfast show was more gentlemanly, I'm sure.

Once in the ring the showman strode out, adding a couple of feet to their stride to keep up with their colt stepping out at the limit of their natural flat walk. There was a fine line between pushing your colt right to the limit of his flat walk without them breaking out into a pace, the flawed version of a running walk described earlier. This is where a little bit of showmanship paid off, making it seem like you were having to really work hard to step out with this colt that seemed to be effortlessly gliding along.

I know I'm making this out to be a really big deal, and to me it was, but a yearling class probably only lasted for fifteen minutes. This was probably the part of the show where most people took a break to find the food trucks or some popcorn. I had worked all day for this fifteen minutes, however, and all I remember was being locked onto that filly. By now I could feel every twitch of anxiety from her and knew how to work her through it. Keep her head moving, subtly talk to her under my breath, step in close to put a shoulder on her neck to steady her, and then give her some room to loosen up and step it out. Three or four laps in one direction, and then three or four in the reverse and it was over. Almost.

For the last part of the contest we were asked to "park out" our colts at one end of the arena. For a yearling this was a way to show discipline in your colt, that they not only could move but they could obey and be still. I won't go into the other reasons behind it because I'll probably get it wrong, but it took a lot of work to get a yearling to learn this stance and have the discipline to maintain it.

The trick was to pull them up facing you and have them back squarely onto their hind legs, and then step forward again and square up their fore legs while keeping their back ends in place. The result was a colt standing proud and high on his front end, chest full, and his back end slightly stretched out behind him. That was half of the trick; the rest of it was getting them to stay perfectly still for about five minutes while the judges inspected each of them. I'm not sure how many shows were won during this phase, but I'm sure a few were lost. A colt that repeatedly stepped out and had to be re-parked over and over or shied away from the judge as he walked all around looking it over, would find himself traveling lower and lower in the judge's order at ribbon time.

I couldn't have been more proud of my filly; she was perfect. That bucking, wild-eyed colt had turned into a real show horse, just as Rocky predicted. By the time we hit that show ring, I don't think she knew there was anyone else around besides me. She listened to everything I asked of her, stepped out just as loose as she could be, eyes straight ahead with one ear cocked to hear my voice. I really didn't know how I was doing compared to anyone else; I don't think I had the wherewithal to look around, but I couldn't have been more pleased with our performance up to that point.

When we parked out, I took a spot at the very end so I would be the last one the judge saw, a trick of showmanship passed down to me by Dad and Rocky. This was a double-edged sword, of course. If the judge already had her high on the list, then saving the best for last had its obvious merits. Being last, however, we had to keep it together the entire time while he looked over each and every colt before us. She stood there like a statue, eyes locked on me, ears perked up high and straight ahead. Perfectly squared up with her hind end stretched back, but not unnaturally so.

We stayed in that position while the judge submitted the results to the announcer. Somehow, I already knew we'd won. I didn't have any real concrete reason to think she'd done any better than everyone else, but I just couldn't have imagined her doing a greater job. Maybe it would have been good for me to come in third or fourth in my first show—it probably would have been a good character building experience—but I'll never know. That night, our number was called first.

Trying to act like I'd been there before, I took her halter in hand and we paraded down the show ring to the winners circle to get our ribbon. She parked out again just like a pro and locked her eyes on me as we posed for a picture. As I look at it again now, she seems like she could go to sleep on her feet right there—and I don't blame her. As we exited the show ring there was praise and neck rubs for the Golden Girl, congratulations to me from Mom and my grandmother, "Baba."

Dad and Granddaddy and all the guys were obviously proud but reserved in their praise, maybe slightly shocked that it worked out like that. I think the fact that I hadn't really considered this a possibility until the very end made it easier to take it in stride. I was just so proud of both of us, the fact that we had a ribbon to show for it was just a bonus.

It wasn't about a blue ribbon, or hearing our name called out over the loudspeaker, or the congratulations and pride from my Harlinsdale family. It was personal pride and satisfaction in the hours and miles and sweat it took to get her to that moment. The entire summer before, learning horsemanship and showmanship, sometimes the hard way. The entire day leading up to the show, endless hours of line working and walking, hours and hours of bonding with this colt until we were basically attached to one another. I don't really care if most of the show audience was in line for a snow cone during that class; all I knew was that we had earned every blue inch of that ribbon.

I took Rebel's Golden Girl back to the trailer; by now she was definitely asleep on her feet. I offered her some water and hay and tied her up outside the trailer to rest, something that just that very morning would have caused her to panic and try and pull the trailer down to run away. Now she just stood there, eyes half closed, as peaceful as could be.

I imagine we stayed for the whole show, through the stakes class at the end which must have wrapped up around 9:30. Finally we loaded up the horses, put away all our grooming supplies, and crawled back into the Chevy to make the trip back to Franklin. Most of the guys lived thirty minutes south of town in Columbia and Spring Hill, so Dad and I graciously offered to take the colts home by ourselves, given that we lived in Franklin only five minutes from the Barn. There is zero chance I made it all the way home without falling asleep sitting up. The smell of that truck would put me to sleep right now, infused with the smell of hay and horses that always sedated me.

Knocked awake by the truck hitting all the potholes coming down the Lane, we pulled up to the Barn and Dad and I unloaded the colts. We gave them fresh hay and some celebratory grain, checked their water and closed up their stalls. Finally home and in bed, it was probably midnight. What a day, more than enough to send a fifteen-year-old boy off to a sound sleep within seconds of hitting the pillow.

The next thing I remembered was being shaken awake by my dad. Not in an anxious sort of way, more like a "Time to get up; what are you still doing in bed?" sort of way. I was so confused, overcome with complete brain fog. This was before I joined the Marines or had children of my own, when I learned that the human body could perform on a shockingly small amount of sleep. It was 6:15 in the morning and I was in serious sleep debt at that age.

The memory of the night before flooded back and woke me up a little, but I was still in a daze. What was going on, and why was I getting up again so early? I was a conquering hero who needed to recover from my trial. My legs and back were still sore from being on my feet so long the day before and my neck had a nasty crook in it from passing out in the truck on the way home. I realized my dad was in his work clothes as he left my room to head down for breakfast, and then it finally hit me.

The show was a Friday night show.
Today was Saturday.
We worked on Saturdays.

Clay Harlin with Coins Double Pride, three days after being knocked unconscious when he was thrown from a horse.

Talbot and Rebel's Golden Girl.

Talbot and Show Sheen at Spring Hill.

Baba and Granddaddy with Talbot, holding the silver cup won with Show Sheen.

Clay and his father Bill, after a win in the yearling class in Shelbyville.

Dan flashes his customary smile, with Clay and Anna Beth, c. 1996.

"We only have good, better, and best."

-Wirt Harlin

The Sale

Dad would've been gone for almost a week by the time Mom piled us kids into the car that Saturday morning and drove us down to C. A. Bobo's "Sellebration" sale grounds just outside of Shelbyville. Dad and the rest of the guys would've spent the week before getting up at 4:30 every morning to get to the sale grounds and start working all the colts. The buyers who would attend the four-day sale were all in town for the Celebration horse show that lasted two weeks, and our yearling auction was timed to get the most attendance by holding it on the Wednesday through Saturday of the second week, culminating during the last two days of the championship show.

 We never called it the "yearling auction," or the Sellebration; it was always just called The Sale. By the time we got there around 9:00 a.m., everyone was down to business, game faces on. There was focus and hustle among the Harlinsdale crew as they got the colts ready for that day's lineup. Each one would have already been worked on a lunge line for an hour, bathed and groomed, taken through a soundness inspection by the veterinarian, and would be standing by in its stall with a show halter and ribbons braided into its mane. No one had any time for small talk, except maybe Dan Ford, who always had time for small talk. Dad would already have a sweat ring around his collar and he and Rocky would be busy tending to last-minute details or chatting up potential buyers.

Around the sale grounds were food vendors selling breakfast biscuits, sandwiches, hot dogs, hamburgers, and barbecue. Trucks and horse trailers and cars parked in rows all around the fields surrounding the arena. The spectator stands probably held about a hundred people, and the arena was about seventy-five feet long and maybe twenty-five feet wide, but in my memory it was about the size of Neyland Stadium. Our colts made up the bulk of the sale but there are a few other barns that we partnered with to fill out the lineup, making it about a hundred yearlings between both days. Timing was important and once the auction started, there was no down time. As soon as the auctioneer's hammer sounded "Sold!" on one horse, the next one was coming right in.

For most of the yearlings, this sale was the first time they had ever been beyond the fence line of Harlinsdale Farm. A select few had been taken to horse shows around the area over the summer, but for the rest this was a world they could have never imagined. They were wild eyed and tuned up, each handler trying his best to appear relaxed as he flexed nearly every muscle in his body to keep his colt under control. Just outside the arena, the next colt on deck would prance in circles in anticipation of entering the arena flanked by more people than they had ever seen in their entire life.

The man in the arena would take his colt down the length at a pace or a walk, doing his best to show off the colt's talent. There were always one or two spare horsemen waiting just at the edge of the arena, ready to tag in and take over after a few laps. The auctioneer, Ray Bennet, would fire off in his machine gun cadence to keep the action going and if the bidding stalled, my grandfather, sitting right beside him, would jump in with some color commentary:

"Aaaaand we're gonna start at fifteen hunnr'd, fifteen hunnr'd, Yes, sir, fifteen, do I have a two, would ya gimme a two, gimme a two, gimme two-thou-san-dollars, Yes, sir! Back to you sir at twenny-five dollabid, gimme-a twenty-five! There's twenny-five, now a three, gimme a three; there's three! Let's go three-n-a-half, three-n-a-half, that's thir-ty-five-hunnr'dollas; gimme thirty-five, thir-ty-five-dolla-bid, thir-ty-five-hunnr'dollas...

"Now listen here folks, this filly is as pretty as they come. She's out of a mare named Coins Delight that won the four-year-old class here at the Celebration in 1992, and her colt last year will be in the two year old stallion class tonight."

In the early days, the place to go for a good Tennessee walking horse was the Wiser Horse Sale in Lewisburg, Tennessee. The breed struggled for a while to find its footing, not having the same fan base as say, a Quarter Horse or a Thoroughbred. As a pleasure horse breed and a show horse, it was really up to the individual as to what they were looking for in a riding horse and, of course, it was up to a horse show judge to determine what made a good show horse. As the breed grew in popularity and a more objective opinion developed about what talent was required to really stand out as a walking horse, the trainers began to take the lead in advising owners on what traits to look for and where to go to find a good horse.

Midnight Sun had been "standing at stud" at Harlinsdale Farm since his back-to-back world championship victories in 1945 and 1946. He produced high quality offspring and people came from near and far to breed their mares to him. He also paired very well with the breeding mares that Wirt and Alex kept at Harlinsdale, and when the time came, they would take their yearlings down to the Wiser Horse Sale like everyone else in the area.

As a breeding farm, Harlinsdale used the process of artificial insemination, something that had a higher likelihood of success and could be done in larger volume than natural breeding. This practice is outlawed in many breeds in order to keep the supply of horses low and their value higher. In the mid 1950s, some other breeders sued Harlinsdale and won, forcing them to stop this practice for a while, although it would eventually become the industry standard.

In 1956, Wirt's brother Alex suffered a heart attack. He survived, but decided to simplify his life and retire to Nashville. He sold his interest in Riverbend, which would have been the southernmost tract of land bordering Harlinsdale, and he made it known to Wirt that he wanted to divest of his interests in the farm. Wirt bought out Alex's share of the land, but as for the livestock, it was agreed that they would settle it all by putting them up for auction. And so it was that all their cattle and all of their jointly owned horses, to include Midnight Sun, were put up for auction in 1956.

Before the sale, however, Wirt entered into a personal agreement with a Mrs. Geraldine Livingston. She was a wealthy woman from down along the Florida-George border, and she had taken a special interest in Midnight Sun. Regardless of who owned him, Geraldine and Wirt agreed that his home should remain at Harlinsdale Farm. Mrs. Livingston purchased him for an undisclosed sum[1] and thus received the proceeds of any future stud fees. Midnight Sun would stay at his home in Franklin and remain oblivious to the financial arrangements made on his behalf. Harlinsdale, in the meantime, would continue to produce offspring from his lineage, and keeping the

---

1 The sale price was around $50,000, although this was never publicly acknowledged.

champion of champions in the Barn would continue to attract new business.

Thus, in 1957, it was time for a fresh start, and the first of many horse auctions were held at Harlinsdale Farm. The first year featured: twenty-two yearlings, a couple of two-year-olds, four weanlings, one "good breeding mare," and two horses listed as "other good mares." The first sale was held on Friday, September 6, 1957, on the Friday before the last day of the Celebration. It was held in the hallway of the Show Barn and the spectators lined the second floor hay loft and catwalks. This was back in an era where nearly everyone smoked, and Wirt was terrified they would burn the Barn down.

The next year it was moved into a tent out on the north side of the Show Barn, solving both the fire hazard issue and creating space to accommodate more spectators. Wirt rented a set of stadium seats and an auctioneer's booth. Colonel Fulton Beasley of Franklin auctioneered and Mr. Hayes sat beside him in the booth. Col. Beasley would tap his hammer just so to create a rhythm, and he was very entertaining for the crowd. Mr. Hayes would introduce each horse and the highlights from their pedigree.

Wirt liked to remember the story of the year they first approached one of the community organizations, like the Lions Club or the Kiwanis Club, to set up a concession stand for the sale. He expected quite a crowd, and he thought there was an opportunity for someone to provide food service while raising some money of their own. As the story goes, someone advertised by mistake that there would be "free food"—and that year had record-breaking attendance, although not for people looking to buy horses.

The misunderstanding was cleared up in subsequent years and along with the hamburgers and hot dogs, people began to come with homemade pies and other goods to sell. Even the local Purity dairy set up a booth to sell milkshakes and ice cream.

The sale grew over time and people began to make the trip to Franklin a regular part of their celebration week schedule. Dad remembers as a boy seeing the long fields on either side of the lane full of parked cars on sale day, and on one occasion they even had a buyer arrive by airplane, landing in one of the long, flat, hayfields behind the main barns. Wirt, Alex, and Mr. Hayes were great salesmen, and really knew how to put on a show and work a crowd.

In 1974, the Harlinsdale sale was invited to join with C. A. Bobo in Unionville, Tennessee, just outside Shelbyville. The Bobos had a covered arena and several long barns to facilitate a horse auction. Its location also made it ideal for buyers who were in town for the horse show but couldn't make the trip to Franklin for the day. The change of venue, however, meant the entire operation had to relocate to the Bobo sale grounds for a week or more, and the guys would all bunk together in a rented house in town so they could be working colts before the sun came up.

Getting the yearlings to the sale was quite a process and consumed almost all the working hours between late June and early August. In the early years—what might be called the "harder, not smarter" years of Harlinsdale—the colts would be turned out as weanlings and never touched until the end of that first full year of life. "Wild and woolly and full of fleas, and never been curried below the knees," these colts were a handful. In the Rocky Jones and Clay Harlin era, they implemented a few "smarter, not harder" changes to the program, and it was around that time when they started breaking the colts in the winter as weanlings.

While this change did give them a running start when they got the colts up again the next summer, they were still turned back out through the winter and spring. This was not simply expedient, it was more or less the secret sauce of Harlinsdale. Our yearlings were generally larger and more hearty than some other bloodlines, due in no small part to the way they were raised. Just like a kid who is encouraged to go out and play, get roughed up, climb and jump and get some scrapes, our yearlings grew tough and strong. The first few days of working colts in late June might have taken a toll on us, but it was an invaluable part of their training to grow up somewhat wild.

On regular weekends, when I would go down to the barn on Saturdays as a boy, the mood was generally light hearted and upbeat. Everyone had a paycheck in his pocket and they were looking forward to the afternoon off and the rest of their weekend. The guys were happy to see me and would accommodate me playing around the barn, even though I was probably in the way. I loved watching my dad at work—and I was of course proud of him—and it looked like they were all having fun. The mood at The Sale, however, was quite a bit different.

I wouldn't realize it until I worked it myself in later years, but those days were probably the hardest two weeks anyone would work at Harlinsdale Farm. It was physically demanding, even more than a regular day at Harlinsdale during colt-breaking season. It was also hard on the nerves, watching people carelessly walk up to and all around the same colts that only a few weeks prior would rear and buck and kick at anything that got near them.

For most of us, these mornings started out like any other day of working colts, but with the added excitement of seeing a few faces we hadn't seen in a while—guys like Matt Doak,

Johnny Haffner, Bubba Hay, and Marty Warren, to name a few. Dan's brother Pat, whose two tours in Vietnam deserve a book of their own, was always around to add to the comic relief along with his older brother.

For the salesmen like Dad and Rocky, they were always on tap to entertain prospective buyers and get out a colt or two, or maybe ten, to suit the interest of each customer. They arguably knew these colts better than anyone, and they would do their best to steer a customer toward what he was looking for. That said, if someone was bound and determined to know better, they certainly wouldn't stand in their way.

Watching the guys run the colts through sale was nothing like watching them work yearlings back at Harlinsdale. The look on their faces was a mix of intense concentration and awareness of danger. They ignored everything happening around them, the crowd, the auctioneer, the bid spotters walking the rails and calling out bids. They felt, sensed, anticipated the reaction of their colts, trying to feel the tension and re-direct that energy forward. Watching their colts' eyes, the movement of their ears, the rhythm of their gait, they constantly assessed their level of control.

There was something else on display at the Sale, something that could not be sold—only earned. It was the last full measure of a years' worth of work, back-breaking days out in the hot summer sun and bitter winters braving the cold rain that turns fields to mud. It was the end result of dozens of bruises and scrapes, rope burns and crushed toes, clothes soaked in sweat and boot soles worn down to the last millimeter of leather. The end of it all was finally in sight, and anyone who had been there before wanted to be there again, to be part of it.

Just like anything from your childhood that seemed larger than life, I felt like I was watching my dad play in the Super

Bowl. Getting to do it myself as a teenager was likewise surreal. I think back on it now and I see old photos and realize how small it was compared to my memories. I drive by the old sale grounds and see them overgrown and falling down, and I just can't square that reality with the way I remembered it. As far as I was concerned, the Celebration horse show was in town because of The Sale, not the other way around, and the real horsemen were those heroes of my childhood in that arena.

The grave of Midnight Sun, the field behind it filled with cars for the yearling auction, c. 1970.

The Show Barn during the yearling auction days, c. 1970.

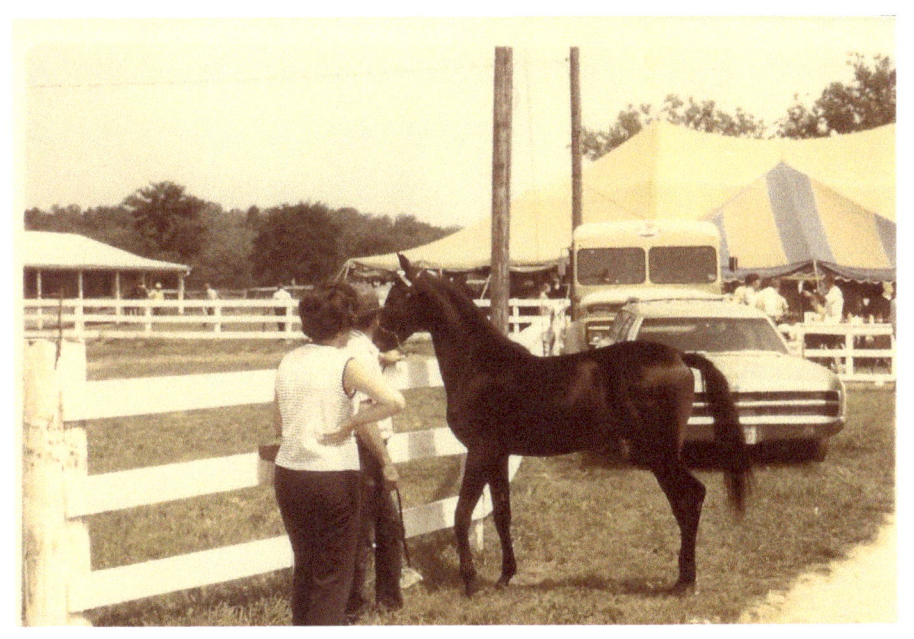

The auction tents in the field in front of the Long Barn, a yearling groomed and ready in the foreground, Purity Dairy truck behind, c. 1970.

Dan Ford is uncharacteristically serious as he bathes a yearling in Shelbyville for the yearling auction at Bobo's sale grounds, 1990.

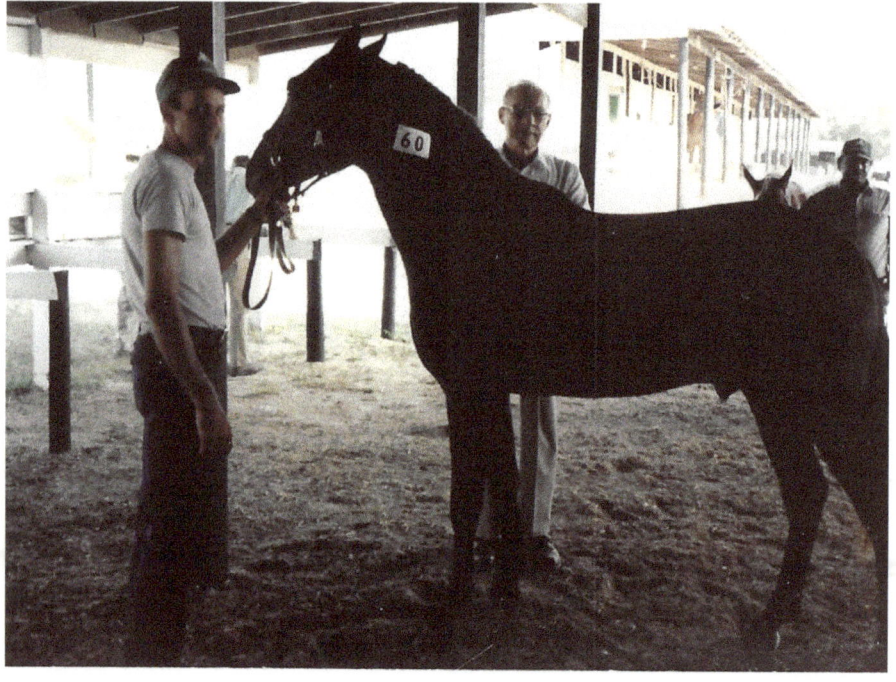

Rocky holds an entry in that day's sale for inspection by the veterinarian; Alfred waits his turn in the background, 1990.

Ray Bennet strikes up his auctioneer's cadence; Bill stands by with commentary, 1990.

Clay leads a yearling into the arena; the rest of the crew stand behind to assist, 1990.

"What did my father give to me? Not an inheritance but a heritage. A sense of sportsmanship that goes far beyond the playing field. He taught me to play fair in everything, and to hate bullies. He taught me good taste and good manners, which have no price but great worth. He opened my mind when I was very young to a love of learning."

-William "Bill" Harlin, Jr.

For Such a Time as This

I told you this wasn't a story about the Tennessee walking horse, and it's not. You could have substituted any breed or any form of equitation into our story and the experience would have been the same. That is, I'm afraid, until the very end—and here we are.

My great-grandfather took my grandfather Bill and his brother Tom to the organizational meeting of the Tennessee Walking Horse Breeders Association at the Lewisburg courthouse in 1935[1]. What began as a gentleman's hobby grew into a multi-billion-dollar industry. In 1944, Wirt and Alex bought their first champion stallion, the four-year old Midnight Sun, for $4,400. In 1999, a four-year-old stud named RPM sold for $1.25 million. Adjusted for inflation, this reflects a relative increase in value of three thousand percent. This type of financial interest in anything—whether it be in show horses, race horses, race cars, or real estate—does not come without corruption.

It started with padded and weighted shoes, or weighted chains around their pastern that people call *action devices*.

---

[1] It is remarkable to note that Wirt Harlin never rode a Tennessee walking horse in a horse show. He liked to joke that the only animal he ever rode in a livestock show was a Hereford bull.

Trainers adopted these methods used by similar breeds to exaggerate a high stepping gait, and the desire to welcome new interest into the breed ran headlong into any desire to keep it pure. When these devices were accepted and became commonplace they were no longer an advantage, so trainers looked for a new angle.

This is where my love of horses and horsemanship hits a roadblock with the "performance horse" show industry. I'll do my best to explain what happened, but I really can't explain why. I'll never completely understand why so many people threw so much money at Big Lick walking horses. I have no earthly idea why anyone would look at a horse and think, "I know what he needs—about four inches of heavy stacked shoes on those front legs. I bet if we really make it harder for him to walk he'll have to wave those front legs around nice and high."

What I'm about to describe is just a snapshot of a practice that is inhumane and immoral. There is no way to live in the light and see it another way. Simply stated, the Big Lick gait is caused by a response to pain. Starting sometime in the 1950s, some trainers—and I'm being very diplomatic by not saying "nearly all trainers"—practiced what is known as "soring." The desire to have the edge on the competition led them to experiment with caustic substances or blistering agents on the fore legs, then wrapping the legs to create a boring sensation deep into the skin.

Once the skin was painfully sensitive, an action device was placed around the inflamed pasterns, resulting in the horse trying to step out and away from the pain. As time went on they found more creative ways to sustain a high stepping gait. They would trim the front hooves down to the edge of live tissue, called *redlining*, before attaching a weighted shoe in a practice known as *pressure shoeing*.

All of this in the name of causing an otherwise perfectly sound animal enough pain to want to keep its fore legs off the ground for as long as possible, because keeping weight on them for any length of time was unbearable. This had the effect of exaggerating the drive from the rear legs, causing the horse to squat lower and deeper and shift more of its weight backward, thus sending its fore legs higher and farther forward. I understand the basic idea of how this worked, but I am by no means an expert and the methods used to inflict pain were as numerous as the trainers who became experts at avoiding detection.

The truly damning part of this practice is that it was all done hand in glove with an effort to conceal it. If it hadn't been so tragic and led to the death of something I loved so much, it would be almost comical. We were concealing this from whom? Ourselves? The entire walking horse industry could be wrapped up as an allegory of my yearling class at the Belfast horse show. While we were consumed in our own insignificant, backward world, the rest of the country was getting a metaphorical snow cone.

The only reason we let this fantasy play on for as long as we did is because, quite frankly, no one else outside of our inconsequential bubble even cared. We were putting on a show for ourselves, creating an outsized value for something that had no real worth. It wasn't rewarding hard work or natural talent, only indifference to pain and an ability to disguise suffering.

Do sport horses suffer injuries going over jumps that result in lameness and sometimes death? Sure. Do race horse trainers mask the symptoms of an unsound horse to enter a race, cause them to tear ligaments and bruise bones, or sometimes even push their horses to heart failure? Yes. But performance Big Lick walking horses are injured as a feature of their training, not a bug. What would you say if I decided to enter a show with a flat shod walking horse but insisted on having a pair of grooms run along beside me and whip his fore legs every time he put one on the ground? Sound like something you'd like to watch? Of course not. So, the industry permitted trainers to do much worse things for the same effect, but politely hid them from the view of spectators who would rather pretend it wasn't happening.

Dr. Johnny Haffner was so conflicted by this practice that he got out of the walking horse business altogether. A video he made while doing a soundness inspection at a horse show in Columbia was used by the trainers to win a court battle against the USDA inspection protocols at horse shows. In this instance, the client who approached him for help knew he had a sound horse and Johnny knew him to be honest, but his attempt to clear this man's name was used as an indictment of the inspection process altogether. When the lawyers deposed him before the trial, he made it clear that if asked about the practice of soring he would not hesitate to tell the truth—that he knew they were doing it.

The lawyers deftly avoided that direct question and the judge decided against the government inspectors in the case. After the inspectors were forced to back off, the abuse became rampant and Johnny couldn't help but feel he had blood on his hands. He was confronted in a moment of clarity by Isaiah 1:15–16, "Your hands are full of blood! Wash and make yourself clean, take your evil deeds out of my sight." He sold his share of the practice in 1992 and has since been a professor at the School of Agriculture at Middle Tennessee State University, among other things, but he would never again be complicit in what he knew to be immoral.

I neither judge nor celebrate people for what makes them ordinary, but for what makes them extraordinary. The practice of soring was so commonplace in the latter half of the twentieth century that it was nothing remarkable. I don't judge the trainers any more than I judge my fourteen-year-old self for feeling the pride of sitting in the box seats at the Celebration labeled "Harlin Family" and watching the horses ride past us in the ring. We were all there, we saw it, and we knew it. It put food on our tables and clothes on our backs and gave us a purpose and a livelihood. What is remarkable, and makes my father extraordinary, is that against his own interest he tried to put an end to it.

In the late '80s and early '90s, Dad began to serve on the Tennessee Walking Horse Breeders and Exhibitors Association board of directors. He served a few consecutive terms as the senior vice-president. During this time, he had various responsibilities and found himself serving as the director of the breeders' division and had a seat on the Walking Horse Commission, which oversaw horse shows and enforced objective standards of judging.

Through the years, Dad and several other members of the new generation of horsemen championed improvements to bring integrity to the walking horse registry. Membership in the association by walking horse owners swelled from ten thousand to twenty-one thousand during this time. They cleaned up most every part of the industry except one. Dad had been preached to his entire life about the corruption that was finding its way into the performance show horses and finally he thought there might be enough new blood in the membership to root out the unsound training practices that had become endemic.

As part of his responsibility on the Walking Horse Commission, he had to consider all the infractions that were brought before the board against trainers who sored their horses so egregiously that a judge actually noticed. Dad understood the nature of the competition; he understood the pressure the trainers were under. He knew if they didn't do it, the owners would just find another trainer who did. He knew if anyone played by the strictest interpretation of the rules, their horses would not win shows and the breeders would exclude their studs from any breeding program. It was a vicious cycle, but he thought he might have a winning tactic.

At the time, and possibly still today, there was no official body that judged horse shows, nor was there an industry-wide standard for horses to pass inspection prior to entry. It would be as if the referees and umpires in professional sports worked for individual ball clubs, instead of answering to the league at large. Sound like something that is ripe for corruption, maybe even bribery? When Dad put this new regulation up for a vote at the TWHBEA board of directors, it failed to pass.

He also championed a program whereby a judge might be able to use an objective standard to determine lameness in the show ring and excuse a horse from the show. No one needed to have his nose rubbed in the reason why; it could be done simply as a courtesy to let an owner see that their horse wasn't sound enough to compete. Everything would be done in the open and the standards would be enforced. This would at least have some deterrent on the worst offenders and might lead to some movement against the practice altogether. At the end of the day, it was a reasonable step that shouldn't have had much push back. Who wouldn't want a judge to excuse a horse from a show that was obviously in pain or nursing an injury?

Well, it turned out a lot of people. Dad was shunned, even yelled at publicly in the hallway of the TWHBEA building by a particularly unsavory trainer, who for all intents and purposes challenged Dad to fight him "out back" to settle the matter. Dad knew there would be some resistance, but he wasn't prepared for what we started to call the "redneck mafia."

The director of the program to bring integrity to horse show judging was fired, the program itself canceled. USDA inspectors, who had been held at bay for years by being told the industry would self-regulate, began to show up in force to inspect horses before shows, but trainers would refuse to submit to inspection or in some cases would boycott the show en masse. Instead of moving the industry in the right direction, the big money and power pushed hard and moved it backward.

Dad had always assumed the core of the industry was basically sound, but was only infected by a small group of bad actors. He was now sick at heart with the sudden realization the infection might be so widespread as to be incurable and potentially fatal.

All this weighed heavy on his heart as he sat on our back porch one Sunday afternoon. It was April 5, 1998. He was taking solace in Scripture, as was his custom. He had just finished a passage in the book of Esther, chapter 4:

"For if you remain silent at this time, relief and deliverance for the Jews will arise from another place, but you and your father's house will perish. And who knows but that you have come to your royal position for such a time as this."

And then the phone rang.

A reporter from the Tennessean had been put onto Dad's trail after interviewing another board member and walking horse trainer. He was working on some background to write a story about why the Walking Horse Trainers Association had boycotted their own show after the USDA showed up with inspectors. He was actually trying to get my grandfather on record to see if he wanted to refute this trainer's assertion that the breeders were just as complicit as the trainers in resisting any reforms to the industry. Instead, he got the one man on the phone who had just been given encouragement from the Almighty Himself to take a determined stand.

Dad didn't say anything accusatory or hateful. He didn't absolve anyone of guilt, nor did he lay the blame on anyone in particular. He acknowledged the mutual sin they had all committed by allowing it to subsist as part of the walking horse business for so long.

The following week on Easter Sunday, April 12, 1998, the story appeared on the front page of the Tennessean, titled "Horseman: It's Gut Check Time." The author quoted Dad as saying, "We've got to choose self-regulation. Either we're going to do it or we're going to have it done for us. The USDA is not playing around. I'm not out to hurt anybody; these are good people and good families. They've gotten stuck in a way of doing things and sometimes maybe a little waking up helps us all. We sort of brought this on ourselves."

Maybe he should have hung up the phone. Maybe he should have had a conference with my grandfather first about how to respond. The truth is, the industry was going to die anyway because it had a terminal illness. Dad only made the mistake of saying it out loud. He showed them that they only had a few years to live and they hated him for it.

Overnight, people who had known Dad his entire life turned their backs on him. People who had done business with Harlinsdale Farm for decades came and took their horses away. At the time, we had several champion stallions "standing at stud" in the Show Barn, and they all were taken away. The owner of our most popular and productive stallion showed up with a trailer one morning and publicly demanded that Dad recount his statement or he would load up his horse and leave with him. Dad refused, and the stud was gone.

In another instance, the much more sympathetic owner of another world champion stallion called Dad privately to explain how all the trainers were going to boycott anyone who had anything to do with Harlinsdale Farm. She felt conflicted and sick about it, but she moved her stud to another breeder anyway.

I'm not sure it's possible for children, even young adults, to sympathize with what their parents have going on in their lives outside of just being parents. I remember this period of time, but I couldn't possibly have appreciated the amount of strain and anguish my father woke up with every morning. This thing he loved so much and the place he had belonged to his entire life, was now the source of so much pain.

No one stepped up to place a shoulder next to Dad's on this hill, not even my grandfather. He continued to go to work every day for a year and a half, knowing that everyone he worked with on and off the farm was privately, or sometimes not so privately, disgusted with him for speaking out of school and shaking up their little world. He wasn't so much like Esther in King Xerxes' court, but like Jonah on a sinking ship lost in a storm. So, like Jonah, he offered himself up as sacrifice.

Dad left the farm in 1999 and went to work running one of my grandfather's businesses out in Tullahoma. This pound of flesh seemed to satisfy some of the most vicious elements of the mob and the attacks against Harlinsdale seemed to abate. There was at least one trainer brave enough to fill the vacuum left by the loss of two of our champion breeding stallions, and the addition of Gen's Major General to the Show Barn would keep the farm on life support for a few more years. Dad would make the drive from Franklin to Tullahoma several times a week, sometimes every day, 114 miles round trip past the very farms and training barns that had worked so hard to force him out of the horse business.

The industry closed ranks and the abuse got worse and the abusers got bolder. People began to pay attention and ask questions, political influence from the Big Lick crowd could no longer keep the Feds at bay. The USDA began to enforce the mandate of the Horse Protection Act with new technology that made it harder for trainers to conceal abuse. Mobile x-rays, thermal imaging, and rapid chemical detection tests made it almost impossible to pass an inspection with a sore'd horse.

In 2006, only three horses passed inspection to enter the final championship class, and for the first time in Celebration history the show was canceled by its own organizers. Incidentally, one of the three who cleanly passed inspection was my grandfather's last show horse, Rowdy Rev, trained and ridden by Bill Bobo.

Over the next decade the walking horse industry, such as it was, imploded. The registry of the Tennessee Walking Horse Breeders and Exhibitors Association declined by ninety percent. The cumulative attendance at all ten days of the Celebration championship show in 2019 was 25,000, a decline in attendance of almost eighty-five percent since 1996, and less than the number of people who used to attend a single championship night at the show's finale. The precipitous decline in demand for yearlings became a running joke that, "if you want a walking horse, just take your horse trailer to Shelbyville and leave it for a minute; when you come back there'll be three or four tied up to it."

Dad was understandably filled with bitterness and anger. Luckily for him, God had just the right therapy—a two-hour commute through walking horse country every day. He and the Lord worked through it, and in time he learned to love his enemies and see God's plan. After six years of running Midsouth Uniform, he turned the business around enough to make it a thorn in the side of a larger competitor and they made an offer to buy it.

Dad was out of a job once again until the door finally opened for him to pursue his true calling as a man of God. He served as the teaching pastor at a church in Brentwood, sharing his immense wealth of knowledge gained from countless hours of Scripture study throughout his life. He was blessed to lead mission trips to Haiti, Honduras, Romania, Ukraine, and India.

I worked on the farm one more summer after Dad left. I joined the Marines right out of high school and served for twenty years, but spent the first four years in the reserves so I could go to college. In the summer of 1999 I was at Parris Island for recruit training, but I came home the summer after my freshman year at the University of Tennessee to work on the farm again.

From my perspective, it seemed the same on a basic level. The stalls still had to be thrown out every day, hay still had to be gotten up from the fields, we still ran a breeding program and yearlings had to be broken. In other ways, nothing was the same. The size of the summer work force was a skeleton of its former self. The lunge circles were a little lonelier, the camaraderie on work details less cheerful, the people who used to drop in around the farm and break up the monotony of the day seemed not to come around anymore.

Most significant to me, my dad wasn't there. As with all things in life, where there is healing there are also scars. In time most of the people who questioned Dad's decision came to honor him with their respect. Some of the very trainers who so viciously attacked him have become the most ardent supporters of the sound horse movement within the industry. But I don't think I'm being dramatic to say that Dad's heart was broken. My perception of reality was shaken, as was my understanding of our place in the world.

I can't say that I ever seriously considered a career at Harlinsdale as part of my future, but I still took it for granted that it would always be there, that it would wait for me and I could come back to it. When I left that last summer to go back to school, a part of me knew Harlinsdale was dying. And now I wish for all the world I could have lingered for a little while longer, as if there were some way for me to make it feel how much it meant to us before its soul was gone forever.

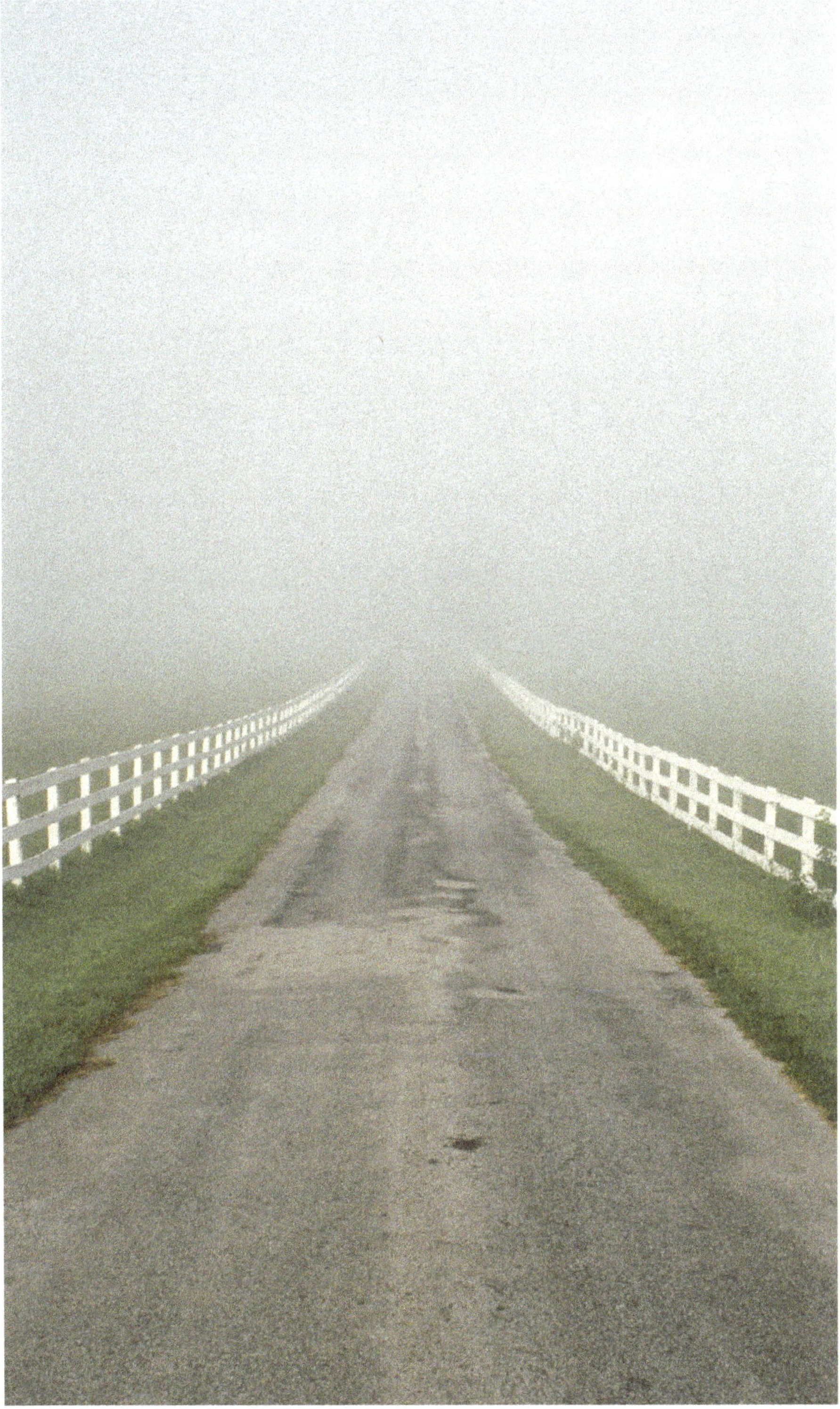

"The tale is told. The world moves on. The sun shines as brightly as before, the flowers bloom as beautifully, the birds sing their carols sweetly, the trees nod and bow their leafy tops as if slumbering in the breeze, the gentle winds fan our brow and kiss our cheek as they pass by, the pale moon sheds her silvery sheen, the blue dome of the sky sparkles with the trembling stars that twinkle and shine and make night beautiful, and the scene melts and gradually disappears forever..."[1]

-Sam Watkins, Company Aytch

---

[1] Sam R. Watkins, *Company Aytch or a Side Show of the Big Show, a memoir of the civil war*, 1882

Elegy

Could these things have happened, been so much of our existence, and then at once be gone? It's still there; I should at least acknowledge that. You can go there now; same as me. It's open to the public during daylight hours and aside from things like the Pilgrimage Festival, in which case you'd have to buy a ticket; same as me. The barns are still there, the fences actually look prettier than we could ever keep them. Most of the inner fences have been removed to create one large, two-hundred-acre pasture. I know I'm supposed to be grateful that it's still there, that it isn't another cookie-cutter Franklin neighborhood or a strip mall with a Pottery Barn next to a Williams-Sonoma standing on ground that we soaked with so much sweat.

My life took me away from Franklin, and Franklin moved on like I was never there, as you might expect. When I first heard the news that Granddaddy was selling the farm, it washed over me like something happening to someone else. Like someone else had been given some bad news and I was obliged to show sympathy for them, but really I had too much going on to slow down and let it sink in. I was just starting out in my military career and after all, there were a few wars on. I repeated the lines I was told—that it was the best thing, that the city would preserve it, that we just couldn't keep it up anymore with the walking horse business the way it was.

There's something about going to Harlinsdale now that just feels out of place. I think the strangest thing is that it's all still there, but somehow it has all been changed. In my memories, the Long Barn had twenty stalls on each side, but now there are only twelve. The Show Barn was more grand than anything of its kind on earth and it held fifty horses, but now there are only eighteen stalls.

It used to be an epic journey to walk down the Lane to the woods up on the Bluff, a journey for which a young boy would need to arm himself with a twenty-gauge shotgun or a .22 rifle before venturing out into the untamed frontier. Now it's just a short stroll people can do with their small children riding in a stroller. The Bluff used to overlook a bend in the Harpeth River from a height of several hundred feet and it took a brave man to step to the edge and look down, but now I think you could climb it without a rope.

I don't get upset when I see all the pictures of strangers at Harlinsdale, the dog parks, the walking trails, even the big concerts. I think it's great, honestly. Even if we'd had the capital and foresight to do something like that with the farm I think it would still feel dead to me. It's good that someone else should find value in it and preserve it.

It's a great place to ride now too, with no fences or gates to open. My wife and I have taken our horses there several times. In a strange sort of sacrilege to my Tennessee walking horse heritage, I had some of my best rides at Harlinsdale on a pair of Thoroughbreds after the city took over our farm and tore down all the fences. I'm not sure what that means, but maybe there's something philosophical about it.

Elegy

I'm older now and have lived a few lives already it seems, more than I deserve. Without making it a prerequisite, I fell in love with a beautiful girl who turned out to share my illogical love of horses. We have two beautiful daughters who will probably bankrupt us with that same affliction. I have had many friends, and still have a few great ones. I have a family who has had hardships and triumphs and somehow we all still love each other.

I think I am finally ready for life to slow down and allow it to sink in—that Harlinsdale is gone. With tears in my eyes as I write this there is finally a deep pain there, but also joy. Gratitude. But that's it, I guess. What we have left is the part that can't be sold. It was our great fortune to play our part in a story that started long ago, through thousands of hard days that made up hundreds of long summers, decades that made up eras, through a hundred years or more and back to a time when we only walked those fields in our grandfathers' dreams.

I am profoundly grateful to God for giving me those years. I am grateful I had the unique opportunity to work next to my father, doing some of the hardest work a man can do. I am grateful for the privilege of sharing hard days with men like Rocky Jones. I am at once grateful and haunted by my love of horses and horsemanship, and not just from a place of romance, remembering only the sweet moments and triumphs. I also remember the pain in my hands, the salt from sweat dried around my eyelids, the frustration of failure—and still I want to go back there.

I want to walk that dusty lane with my dad again, halfway through a day with as much work before us as behind. I want another day in the hayfield, standing on that swaying wagon in the heat. I want to open another stall door and see my next colt challenge me to try and catch him.

I want to collapse into one of those chairs in the hallway of the Show Barn at the end of a long, hard day. All the work is done, horses fed, all the bits of hay swept from the barn floor. Tractors put away, all the mares and colts put up in their stalls, scoops and forks all stowed in the closet. Breeding room cleaned and sanitized, all the buckets and stainless steel counters shining. All the lunge lines coiled up and hung on the wall, hay stacked out at the Long Barn for the next day, gates closed and stall door latches, all checked secure. The Show Barn hallway raked clean and sprayed down to keep the dust settled.

One by one everyone takes a seat or leans against the wall as the breeze flows through the barn. Skin prickly with dried sweat, suddenly you get a chill from being out of the heat and sun. There's Dan Ford and Ben Bowman cracking jokes. Dave Parrish and Oscar Pruitt leaning up against the wall, afraid to sit down for fear of getting too stocked up and stiff to walk home. Al Irwin and Alfred Perkins wiping their foreheads with a handkerchief, commenting to no one in particular, "Boy, it sure was hot today."

Johnny Haffner drops in and visits for a while as we wrap things up. Mr. Hayes steps out of the office and looks like he's almost about to smile, but then thinks better of it. Dad and Rocky stand by the open entrance of the barn and stare up the Lane, arms crossed while silently lost in thought. Both men knowing that all the work is done but neither man willing to be the first to admit that it's time to go home. No one really needs to say anything, just sit and be content in the satisfaction that comes with putting a hard day behind you. It's not worth dwelling on anyway; God willing we're gonna get to do it all again tomorrow.

"This is what I have observed to be good: that it is appropriate for a person to eat, to drink and to find satisfaction in their toilsome labor under the sun during the few days of God has given them—for this is their lot. Moreover, when God gives someone wealth and possessions, and the ability to enjoy them, to accept their lot and be happy in their toil—this is a gift from God. They seldom reflect on the days of their life, because God keeps them occupied with a gladness of heart.

Ecclesiastes 5:18-20

252

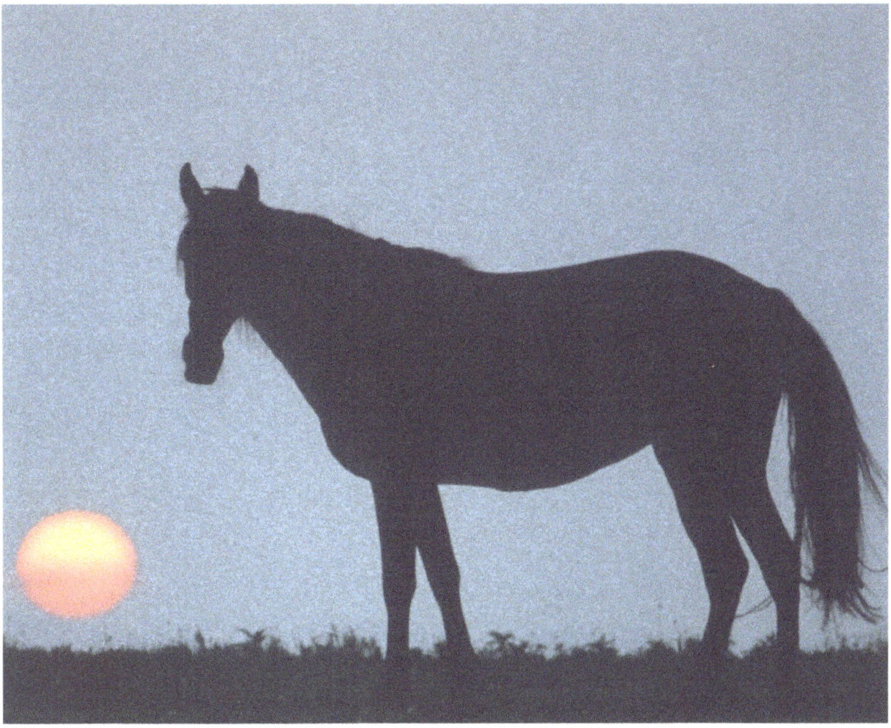

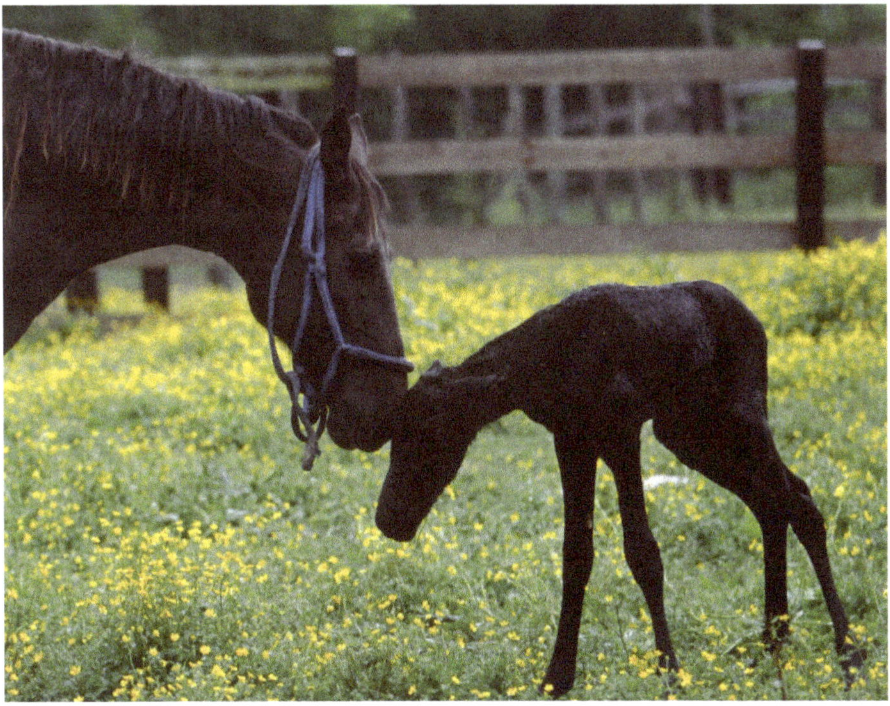

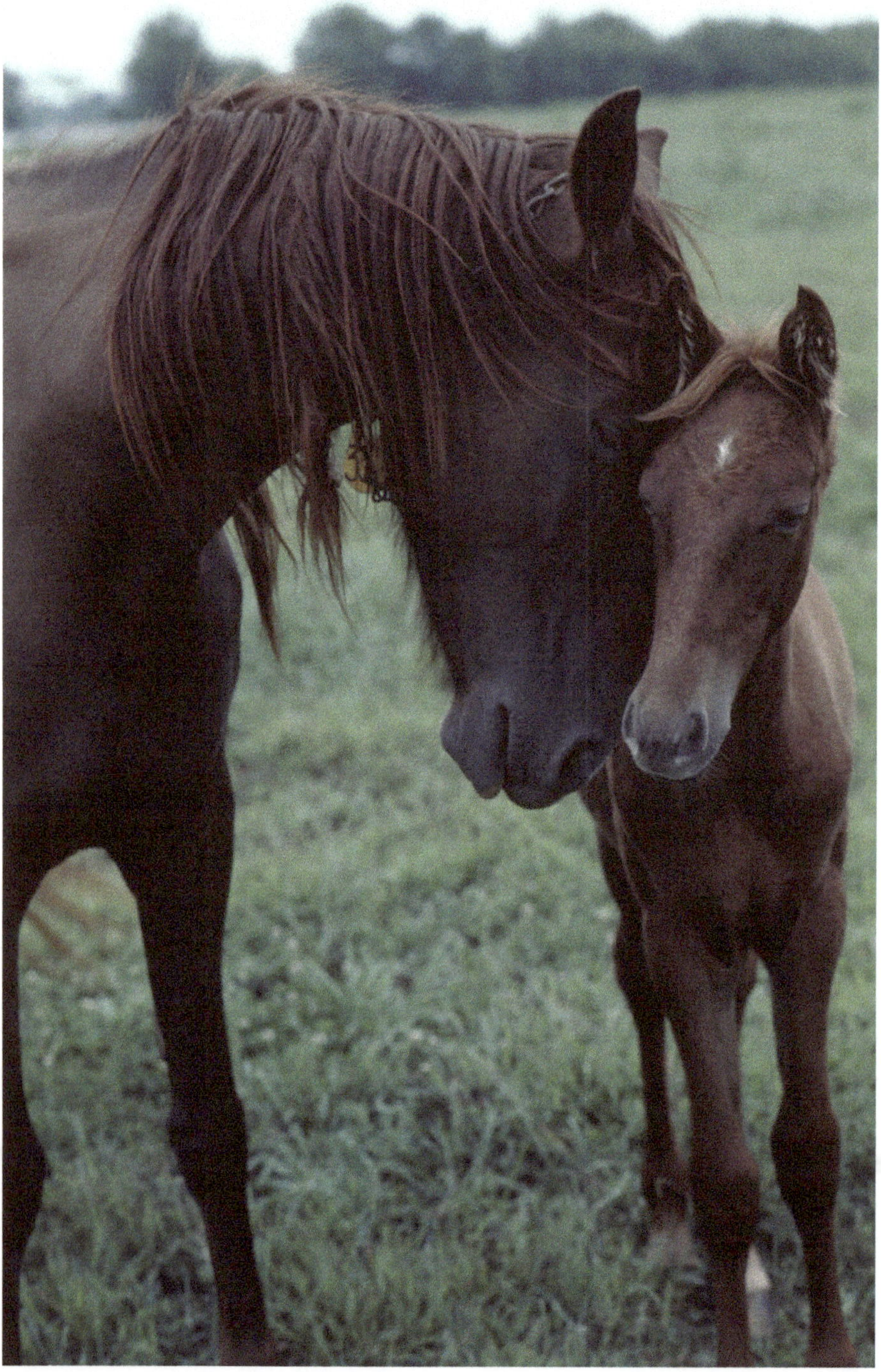

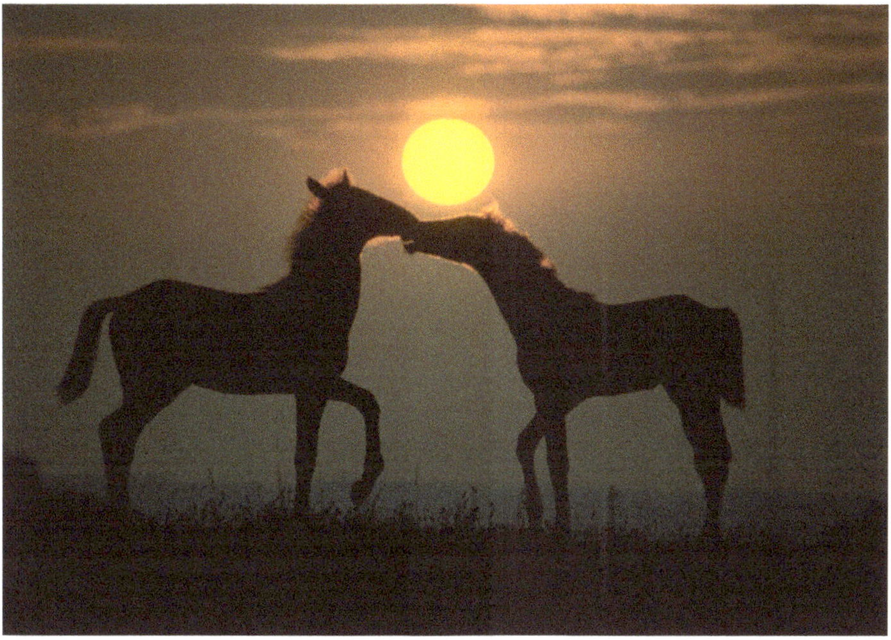

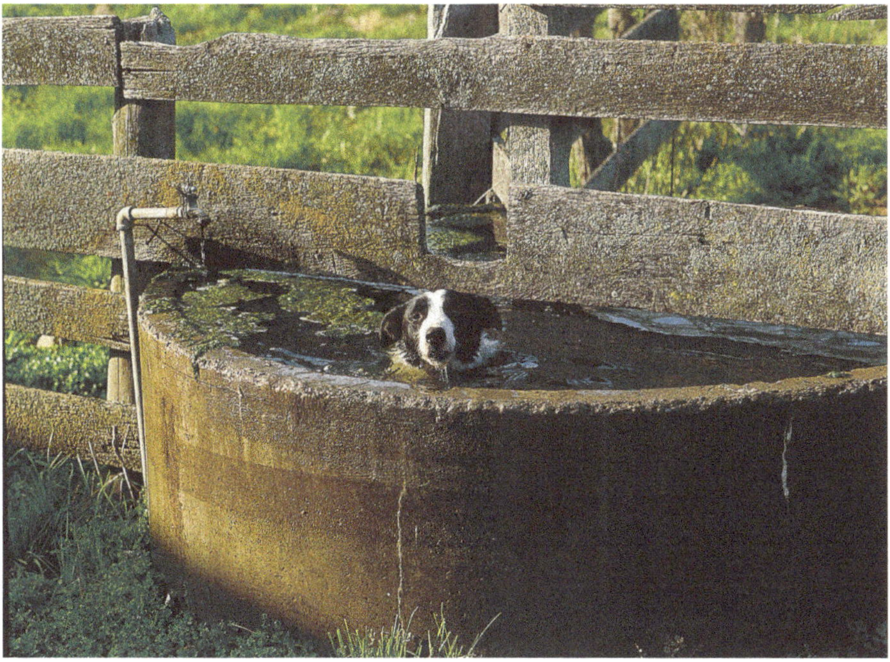

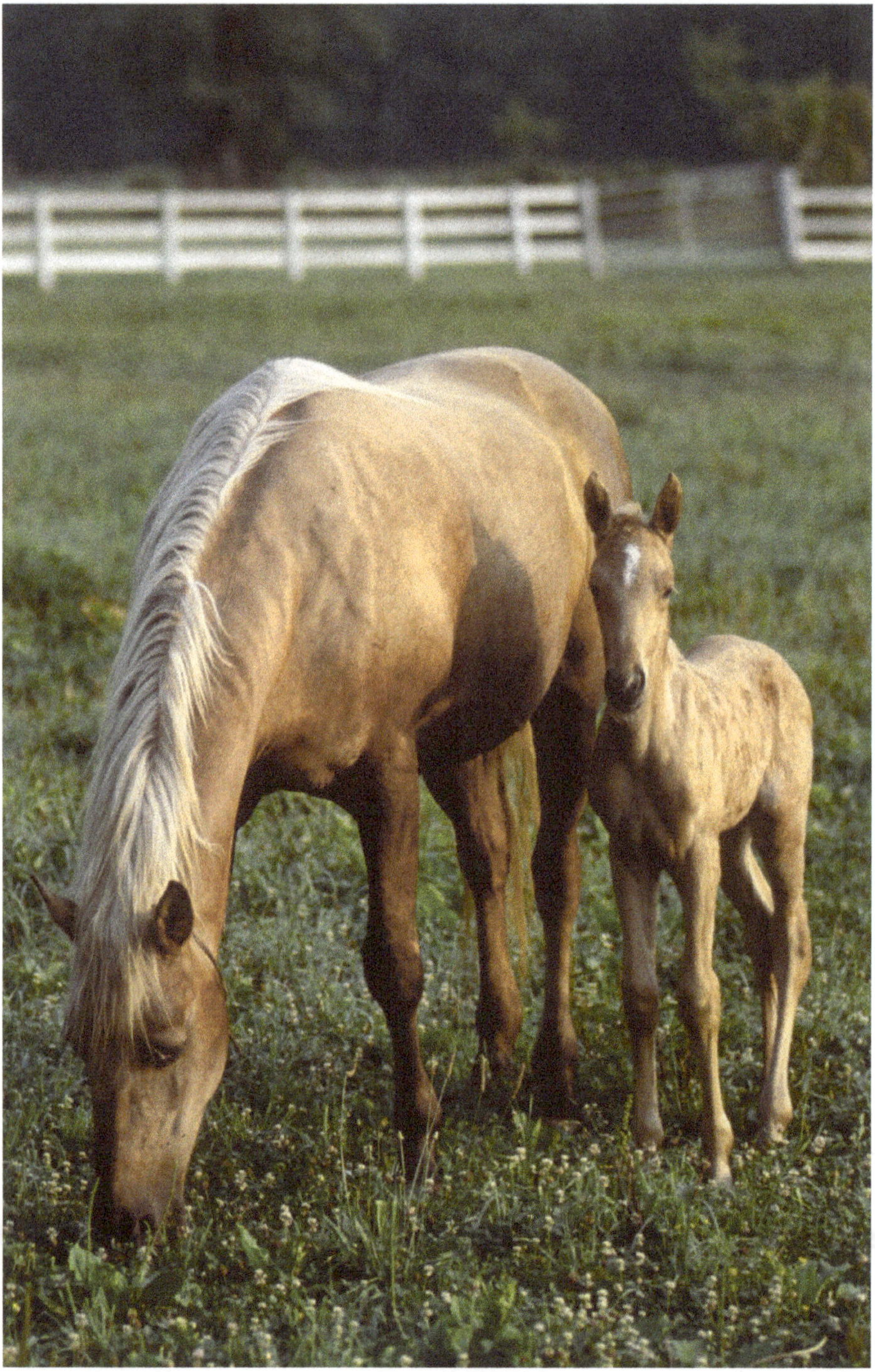

257

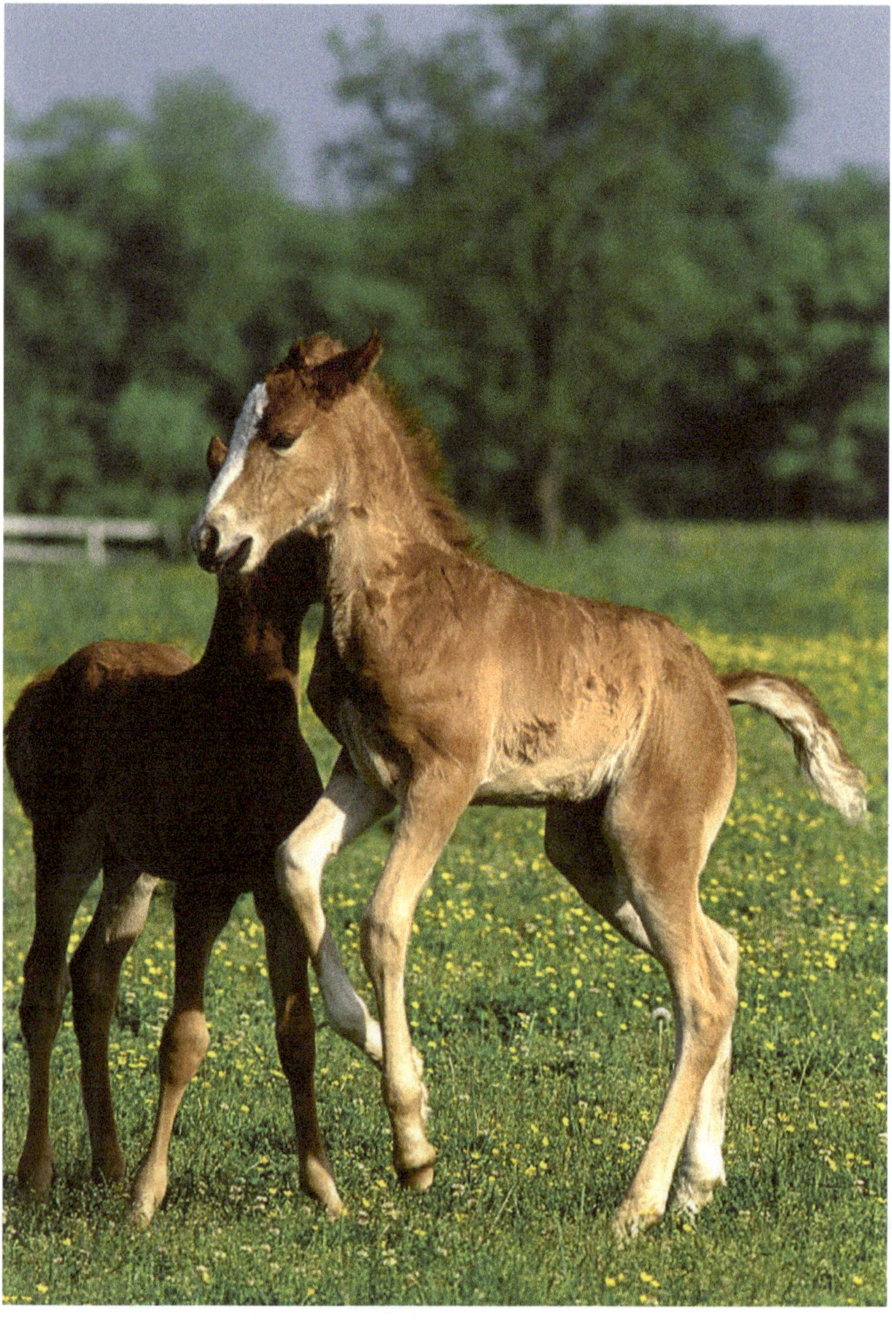

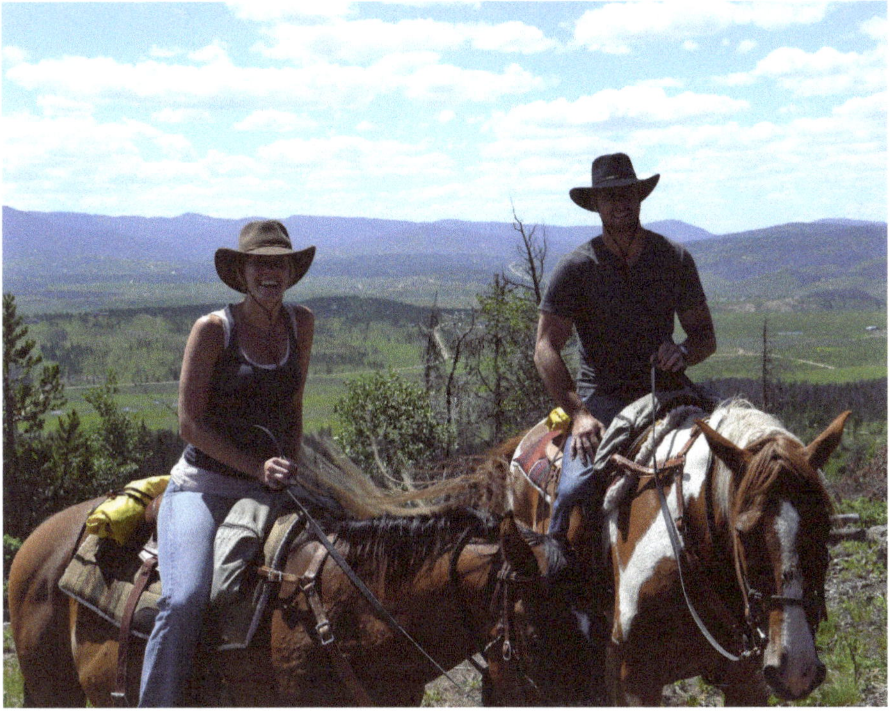

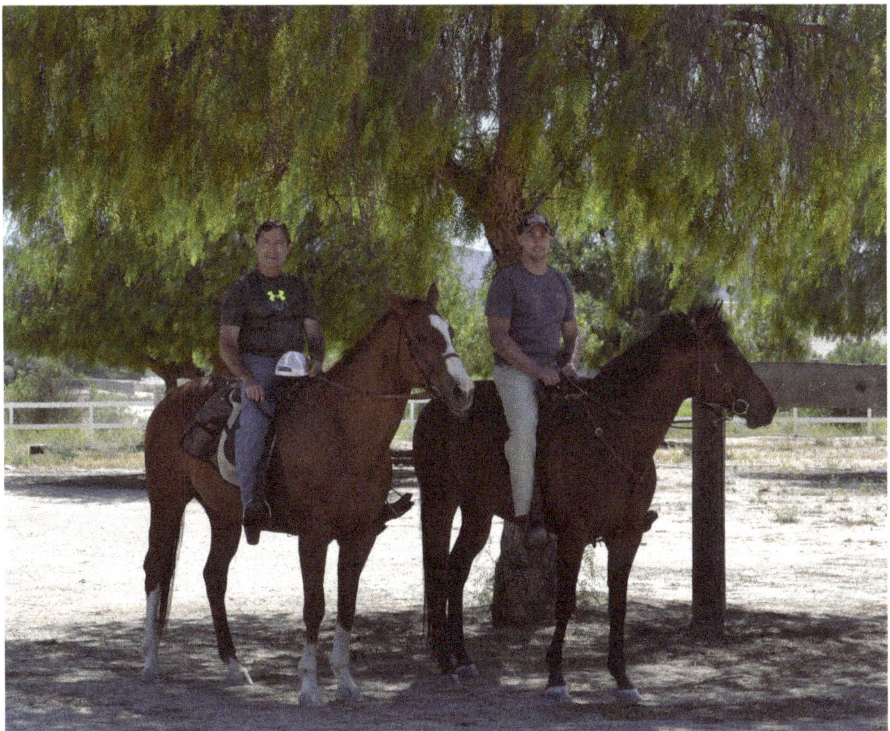

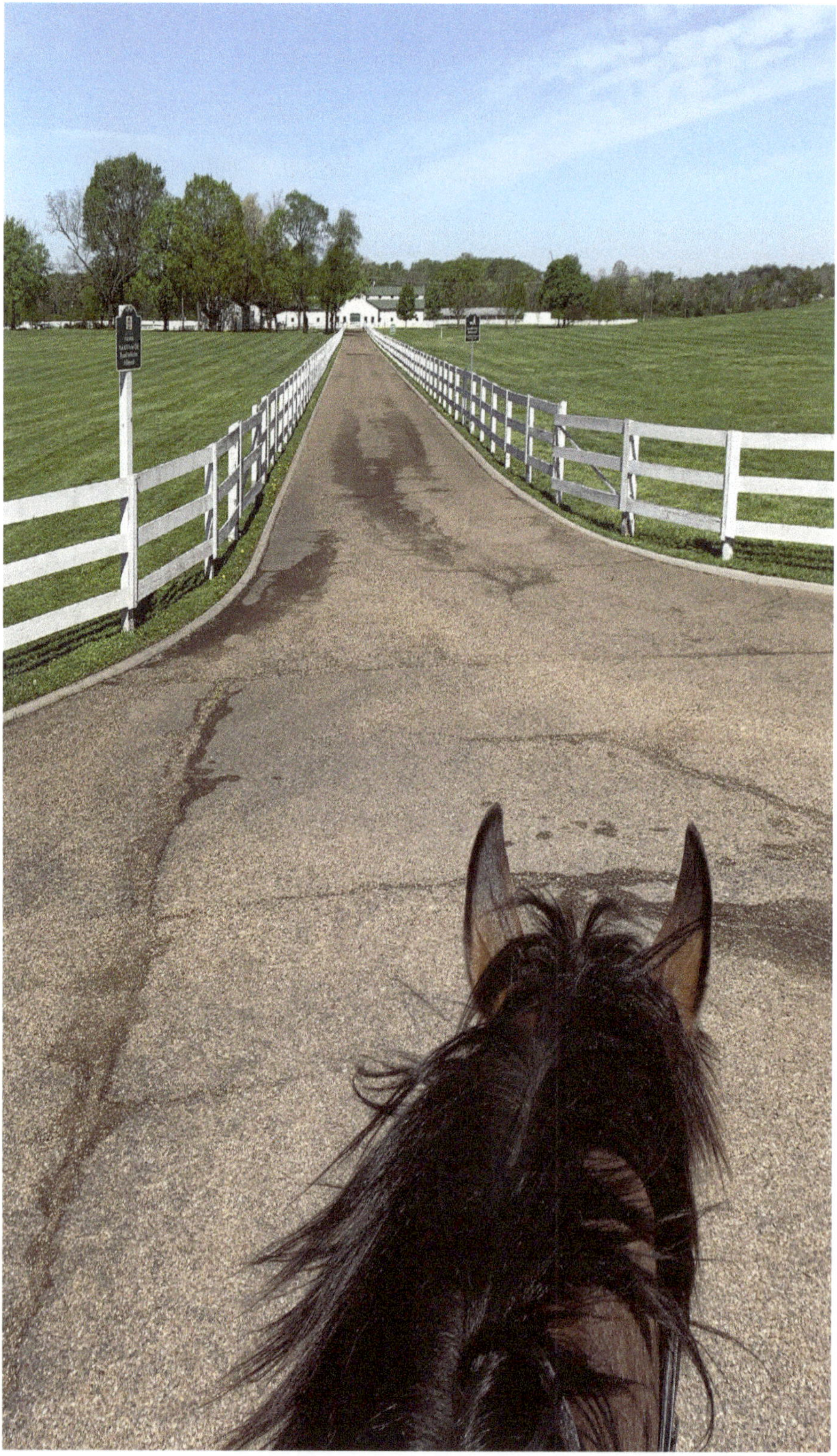

For more of the story, please visit:

HarlinsdaleFarm.com

Milton Keynes UK
Ingram Content Group UK Ltd.
UKHW020639120824
446622UK00005B/79/J